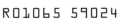

Master Guide to Psychism

Master Guide to Psychism

Harriet A. Boswell

PARKER PUBLISHING COMPANY, INC.
WEST NYACK, N.Y.

Second printing........ October, 1970

*Dedicated to those seeking
heightened awareness for daily living*

What This Book

Can Do for You

The Dark Ages of Psychism are a thing of the past. Fear and superstition are the indications of failure to keep up with the understanding of one's emerging psychic power potentials. If you want to make definite progress in this present Age of Psychic Enlightenment, there is no time to lose—and here in this book are the simple steps that you can take for fulfillment in demonstrating your inborn psychic gifts.

The various uses of mysticism for psychic demonstration have outlived their usefulness in the fields of understanding psychic phenomena—and how to use them practically. It is no longer necessary for you to marvel at the psychic or parapsychological accomplishments of the "informed few." With this book, you can now join the ranks of the "informed many."

Many words have been spoken in the past regarding the subject of psychism, as well as many books published about it. Hundreds of "teachers" have been forthcoming in every decade testifying to the attainment of psychic powers by individuals. Carefully worded phrases, spoken and written, have served to whet one's appetite for psychic power, but they seemingly obscured the real access to one's potentials to demonstrate inherent psychic abilities.

For example, for many years we were taught that the human aura was a sight reserved only for the highly gifted psychically. It is comparatively recently that it was openly said that everyone has an aura. Now, much is known about what a psychic aura is, and how it can be readily seen and used beneficially by all. With a little

7

practice, as set out in this book, you can see your own aura as well as that of others.

You are both a receiving and sending radio, a television set from a psychic point of view, and it is important you understand this principle of psychic communication. For centuries, this carefully kept secret was preserved to serve certain purposes of mystic power groups. It is to your advantage, as set down in this book, to know that *you* can control, and *be* controlled through many psychic means.

This book will prevent you from falling into the trap of attributing the "unexplained" psychic, or "unusual experience" to coincidence, imagination, or "bad" nerves. Further, it will enable you to recognize psychic or "unexplained" phenomena when you may be confronted by a wide variety of parapsychological or psychic experiences.

Spontaneous manifestations of psychic forces are interesting and helpful. However, with this book you can gain much more for daily living by producing certain desired results through psychic means, understanding and direction of the forces of psychism in their limitless applications to your life.

Here is a book concerning your psychic powers that you can understand and apply no matter how much of a novice you may be. You can put the psychic laws and programs into immediate action to test the present level of your psychic awareness and demonstration. All this can lead you to experience definite and concrete benefits in your daily living that you may not have thought possible before you had possession of this book.

THE AUTHOR

Contents

4. THE REALITY OF HUMAN AURAS (*continued*)

5. PREMONITION AND PRECOGNITION THROUGH PSYCHISM 73

6. PSYCHOKINESIS AND TELEKINESIS—POWER OF MIND OVER MATTER 85

ONE

The Path to

Psychic Understanding

and Demonstration

Until excavators unearthed the ruins of many cities and well-preserved relics of long-gone civilizations referred to in ancient writings, including the Holy Bible, there was a large number of skeptics who maintained that these writings were myths believed only by the gullible. Now that the hard core of this brand of skepticism has been cracked, the work of excavating the wondrous psychic gifts within each of us should be begun. Until more people firmly take the time and responsibility to explore their own psychic capacities, to dig through the materialistic concepts with which so much of the world has buried the spiritual part of man, psychic sensitivity for help in daily living will remain in the area of the mythical for far too many.

THE SEARCH BEGINS WITH ONE'S SELF

Each person who has the initiative and the spirit of quest in him can do his part by working with himself first. If his belief in God (or whatever he calls Creative Intelligence) and the wonders of creation is not limited by the idea that we must blunder along in the footsteps of tradition, and if his interest in his fellow-man is such that he wants to do his part, he can reach a state of individual attainment hitherto unsuspected of being within his reach.

Most progress of civilization has been on a materialistic level—better caves in which to live, mechanized tools with which to work, faster means of transporting bodies and materials, effortless communication, body care and health practices which call upon the inner man to contribute little. The benefits thus derived, instead of inspiring mankind to a more avid search for the Great Power which makes all this possible, have created a state of placidity and a decline of personal refinement, a lassitude in the quest for man's understanding of his own higher psychic self.

How materialistic appetites affect psychic progress

As the materialistic appetites of man are satisfied, he has less desire to create great works and develop those spiritual and mental gifts which God has given him for his individual use. What is now needed is less absorption with progress and exploration in the externals, and more attention given to the tremendous power sources in man's inner world. His individual mind and the natural laws governing the realization of mind potential must be brought into a more healthy balance in physical and spiritual areas. The overbalance of materialistic accomplishments has bettered only truly balanced people. It has seriously jeopardized the health, happiness and initiative of the spiritually weak or spiritually unaware.

Is the new frontier of science the hope for the unfortunate majority? Perhaps scientific recognition of the non-physical part of man will result in an increase in man's curiosity about himself and what he is. How insignificant man is in a materialistic concept, and how staggering his importance in a concept that recognizes his individual place in a world that acknowledges his oneness with God!

Francis Bacon said that only a person of limited knowledge could be atheistic because deepening understanding must lead to a belief in a Creator, an intelligence greater than his own.

We are instruments expressing the Creative Mind of God—in a sense we are creators ourselves. Why not sensitize ourselves so that we can receive and express the higher creative impressions which emanate from the source of all things? All of the great art, music, literature and inventions are expressions of the highest sensitivity to inspiration. An awareness and appreciation of this kind of contact, and the manifestation of it in other people, must certainly stand as an experience beyond comparison.

WHAT A NEW SENSE OF AWARENESS CAN BRING

We deny ourselves even the emotional uplift of awareness of the beauty of simple things. Beauty is often unappreciated because sensitivity to it has been dulled in the pursuit of the material. True, we are living in a physical world where material needs must be met, but who, in the pursuit of the material, cannot as he goes observe trees, birds, flowers, the sky, or some part of the natural beauty all around him? Even a city-dweller can glimpse the sky—an awe-inspiring sight if he will take a moment to *feel* it. Too often his only thoughts as he looks are limited to something such as: "Looks like rain, so I'd better take my umbrella," or "Those clouds look as if we might have some snow, which means it's back to the snow shovel again!"

Fortunately something occasionally happens to pique the curiosity of even the most lethargic mind; such as, the discovery of the Dead Sea Scrolls, "flying saucer" sightings, space shots or explorations, and experiments of a startling nature. But much of the knowledge uncovered and many of the theories propounded by scholars and experts are repressed. Why? We are told that man is not yet ready to receive this information.

Unfortunately there is much merit to this argument about man's unfitness to be informed. The vast majority of people today would not be able to cope with the revelations. Man has too long neglected the most noble part of himself and so is unsure of his purpose and uncertain of his place. At the same time, it is equally true that almost unlimited funds are available for more exploration to uncover even more information to add to the storehouse of knowledge of limited usefulness. If man cannot understand it, why should he seek it? Why not have a more equal balance of development? Why not encourage inner exploration so that the outer explorations make more sense?

It is true in a sense that we are not really individuals; we are component parts of a great whole. Nonetheless, we are individuals in this respect: a clock is made up of many parts, each part with its own particular function which contributes to the usefulness and efficiency of the clock's operation. To the same extent that a gear cannot perform the function of a spring, nor that of a gear larger or smaller than itself or out of its proper place, we do not perform our individual functions in the scheme of existence if we do not understand what we are, where we belong and what we are to do. The discovery of these important points is our individual responsibility. We must each discover for ourselves, from the Great Clockmaker, what component part we are. Psychic awareness is the practical answer.

Man carefully fertilizes, mows and waters his yard; he polishes, lubricates and cares for his car; he works for, counts and spends his money; he paints, repairs and maintains his home; he selects, matches and cleans his clothes; he tries to see to it that his food, rest and amusements are properly suited to his physical well-being. Where is his sense of proportion if he will not do as much for his psychic consciousness?

Until man consciously accepts his own relationship to the original Creative Intelligence, by whatever name he might call it, understanding that this is where he can find his imperishable assets, he is only half-alive. To be wholly alive he must have psychic awareness.

Even to say that there is no other God than man, is an expression of man's recognition of a Supreme Being of some sort, since we cannot conceive of or deny anything that does not have some possibility of existence. It is the staggering creativeness of this Intelligence which accounts for the differences, not only between man and other forms of life, but individual diversities within mankind itself. It is the spark of the supreme Creator innate in each of us that makes us individual in talents, personalities, etc. We each create ourselves in expression according to our own sense of value, initiative and, in a way, adventuresomeness. Without this "spiritual" part, we would reproduce almost unidentifiable prototypes.

CONSCIOUS AWARENESS

Everyone must acknowledge that in the human race, at least, there is a vast difference in expression. Something so noticeable must have a name; let's call it conscious awareness. This consciousness manifests its differences in countless ways; there is no doubt that some of the differences may be traced to something physical; also, some of the results of these differences may manifest in a physical way. Those differences which are not physically motivated are the ones which need exploring, since they are not only the predominant differences, but they are also the most mystifying.

For political, economic or religious reasons, it was not considered feasible to encourage man to be fully cognizant of his own individual relationship to God. He was kept in ignorance of the spiritual gifts dormant within him; he was not encouraged to consider himself functioning *among* his peers but *under* his superiors in governmental, business or spiritual "beingness." Without the awesome barriers and the resulting unquestioned superiority of one faction, mankind in general would have shed its acceptance of tyranny. It was imperative that ignorance of potential equality be kept at a minimum. Only a few insurrectionists, such as Jesus Christ, Buddha and other great religious lights, dared to offer enlightenment and freedom to the common man.

The great teachers who made attempts to elevate every man to his rightful place emphasized the necessity of self-realization. Ridicule or worse was leveled at those who dared demonstrate to any degree those great equalizers—the gifts of spirit. It is only in our own time that any attempt is made to recognize these wonderful gifts and to encourage their cultivation and use. Precognition, wisdom, healing, telepathy, inspirational works—these are but a few of the wonders that are buried deep within even the least of us.

By seeking within, developing the psychic consciousness found there, you can become aware of the part of you which is nonphysical. When you are not aware of that part of your inner self which is capable of demonstrating at least one of the nine gifts of spirit which God gave man, you are violating the best part of yourself—the divine part of your nature.

Herein lies your greatest potential, its achievement, and your richest source of satisfaction, once you acknowledge its presence.

PARTICIPATION IS THE KEY TO PSYCHIC DEMONSTRATION

Because of the nature of this book I do not apologize for the fact that the ideas, experiences and programs set out are not literally "scientific" in nature. What is popularly called "science" rejects, for the most part, the whole idea of psychism as either unproven or unprovable. Those who have pioneered in the attempt to turn parapsychology, psychism and other heretofore-designated pseudosciences into the respectable area of true science by careful and intelligent *exploration,* have succeeded in removing some of the stigma from these names.

More than 30 years of my life have been spent in the study of the occult. For most of these years, the use of the word "occult" in discussing my interests brought reactions ranging from raised eyebrows to frightened recoil. This is, perhaps, one of the most sadly misunderstood words in our language. Literally, it simply means "concealed from knowledge or understanding," and applies to *anything* unknown. As Stewart Edward White says in the first chapter of *The Betty Book,* all advancement in knowledge and understanding has been a process of de-occultization.

The first 24 years of my attempt to understand this elusive and tantalizing part of man's makeup was on a purely intellectual basis. I was *studying,* not *participating.* Now I am sure that the objective approach is only partially satisfying. One must become subjective in order to *know.* Truth is such an individual thing—we can believe only that which we accept as valid by our own personal standards. Our truths are determined through experiences, either spiritual, emotional or physical. Occasionally we accept as truth an objective observation, but generally the subjective is more definite and satisfying. We do not nourish our physical bodies by watching someone else eat, no matter how elaborate the meal, nor should we expect to do otherwise with our mental or spiritual "bodies."

The language of most written material available to the layman interested in discovering his own capabilities is difficult because of pedantic style, dull because of statistical coldness, or made unbelievable in an attempt to entertain and amuse. In 30 years of reading I have found few books which proved to be instructive, believable *and* readable. The experiments included in this book all *work,* as has been proven to study groups over and over again; the experiences included are all verifiable; the language is simple and understandable.

We must each make our own way at our own rate of speed to enjoy the treasures we find buried within ourselves. We may pass along our experiences and convey some of the upliftment and wonder we feel, in a limited way; but the greatest benefit is from *experiencing for ourselves* and helping others find the way to do the same. Vicarious adventures are for the timid. Why not explore the wonders of psychism a few minutes each day? Remember that self is the integration of man, and the only way to "know thyself" is to study and apply until you recognize all phases of the whole that is YOU.

SUMMARY OF CHAPTER ONE

1. Psychic awareness is the key to discovering your place in Infinite Intelligence.
2. Why materialistic appetites interfere with psychic progress.
3. The true meaning of conscious awareness.
4. Active participation is the key to psychic demonstration.
5. The benefits of exploring the wonders of psychism.

How to Develop

Your Powers of

Psychism and Mediumship

A dictionary states that "psychic ability in its less sensational way of expression manifests daily to everyone." In its broadest term, "psychic" pertains to the mind or soul as distinguished from the physical or psychological. A tighter definition renders it "of or pertaining to mental phenomena beyond or from non-material forces." And again, "sensitive to mental or occult phenomena." As a noun, the meaning is given as "a person sensitive to mental or extrasensory phenomena; especially a spiritualistic medium."

EVERYONE POSSESSES PSYCHIC SENSITIVITY

All mediums are psychic, but not all psychics are mediums. Heretofore psychism was considered to be a fairly rare attribute, but research seems to indicate that everyone is born with psychic sensitivity which diminishes as time passes. It still exists but does not manifest to its fullest unless the individual understands what it is and practices using the ability. Mediums are merely highly sensitive psychics, either through deliberate cultivation, retention of the ability due to encouragement and understanding during the formative years, or endowment with such a degree of sensitivity that it persists or manifests more or less spontaneously.

Mental and physical phases

Mediumship and psychism have two phases, mental and physical. Physical mediumship is that type which has some relationship to, or effect on, physical things. Mental mediumship is that which pertains primarily to impressionistic material being received. Classified under physical manifestations are table-tilting, apports, Ouija boards, materializations, etc. Mental mediumship pertains to such phases of psychism as clairvoyance (seeing), clairaudience (hearing), clairsenscience (sensing), telepathy, and so on—in precognitive and retrocognitive terms as well as the present.

Trance and conscious categories

Aside from the two main divisions just mentioned, there are two other general classifications: trance and conscious. In the trance category there are numerous degrees of trance, but generally "deep trance" and "semi-trance" are the two terms most frequently used.

DIFFERENCE BETWEEN MEDIUMS AND PSYCHICS

According to spiritualistic views, a medium is a psychic who is so sensitive to high vibrations that he, or she, is subject to control by disembodied spirits. A psychic of lesser sensitivity is generally supposed to be sensitive to vibrations of a lower frequency, such as thought waves or auric emanations. The religionists in the spirit-control field of thought believe that a medium who does not maintain strict rules pertaining to mental, physical and spiritual well-being is laying himself wide open to control by earthbound, or base, entities resulting in manifestations of a very questionable or violent nature. It is for this reason that many mediums are not acceptable to some spiritualist churches.

It is my personal opinion that a serious attitude, strongly positive, and of good intent, is conducive of the highest quality of manifestation. My only upsetting or unpleasant experiences during seances were in the presence of fraudulent or commercial mediums. With the passing of time my reaction to such persons has progressed from queasiness to active nausea before the first few minutes of a seance have passed. I can't explain it—I just have to be alert to early signs and excuse myself before the doors are closed.

QUALIFICATIONS FOR MEDIUMSHIP

Open-mindedness and a willingness to cooperate within the realm of reason are necessary on the part of the sitter. A sensible attitude does not imply gullibility. There is a middle ground between gullibility and hostile skepticism. A calm state of nerves, an ability to discriminate impartially between what is evidential and what is completely irrelevant, plus an impersonal, non-biased willingness to allow the medium to demonstrate his or her capability is imperative.

Obvious fraud betrays itself given time and trial. It is true that many mediums are a mixture of genuine psychic power and either deliberate or unconscious misinformation. It seems to me that the demanding public is responsible for much of the "filling in" which constitutes this type of activity. Some sitters expect results beyond the capacity of even the greatest of psychics. There is no infallible "switch" by which this power may be turned on and off and which can assure a full flow of exactly what sitters expect and want to hear. There is perhaps no field of activity where malpractice is more unforgivable and error so uncharitably criticized than in the field of psychism. Mediums *are* human beings and as such are susceptible to all human weaknesses and temptations. There are fraudulent mediums; there are fraudulent businessmen in all occupations and professions. A person who is basically dishonest will so conduct himself in any endeavor.

Integrity will also prove itself. It has been my great privilege and pleasure to sit with honest psychics and mediums who have made me *know* that some form of communication beyond physical explanation is possible. This more than compensates for the questionable and, I might add, more numerous contacts which have displeased me. Some of the most conclusive material I have received, or witnessed being given to someone else, came from mediums who are quiet, unassuming, non-public mediums who read only for friends and will accept no fee. I do not mean to imply here that in order to be good a medium must work without charge—I think it only fair that a person who devotes the time and effort necessary to be a fine medium is as much entitled to a fee from those benefiting from his "gift" as is a fine musician or artist who shares his gift with the general public.

Many fine mediums do work without set fees involved, but these usually do limit their services in order to protect themselves from publicity and unreasonable demands upon their time and privacy. Some of them do go along with the idea that commercializing will diminish or destroy their gift. This is understandable when one reads the history of psychical research which abounds with accounts of psychics who lost all abilities while under the terrible pressure of functioning as public property.

WHY MANY GIFTED MEDIUMS DO NOT SUBMIT TO TESTING

It is true that scientific rules and test conditions have exposed fraud; but it is also true that many gifted mediums would not be willing to subject themselves to testing under conditions unfamiliar to them, in strange surroundings, and/or the "let's see you prove it" atmosphere so often prevalent or implied in such tests. None of us can function at our best when we are working with the wrong tools, under strange conditions, with a supervisor "looking over our shoulder" for the first sign of uncertainty or error, or in an atmosphere which is expectant of our ultimate failure regardless of our skill in our own environment and under our own conditions. The best of us are apt to lose some of our poise when we are put to a test of our capabilities, so that bluff, exaggeration, error, and even misrepresentation are often resorted to in selling, job applications, examinations, etc.

A medium who depends upon his life of service for his living expenses has much to lose by announcing that "there is nothing coming through" after people have taken the time and paid the fee for a seance, unless all of the sitters are well enough versed in psychical work to accept gracefully the fact that conditions might be unfavorable for obtaining good results. (I seriously doubt whether the skeptics would object to similar delay by a doctor, paying for several office calls before a correct diagnosis could be given.)

Different conditions affect different mediums. Atmospheric conditions can be disturbing to some—turbulent weather or oppressively heavy air may cut off the contact with the necessary vibrations. Hostility, anger or other similar emotions on the part of the sitter may be a deterrent. One should never lose sight of the fact that these are *people* with whom one is dealing, and they are just as subject to moodiness and emotional reactions as anyone else. Regardless of the cause of failure, mediums are well aware of the fact that an announcement of inability to produce generally is more apt to draw unwarranted criticism or unfair reactions toward them than the average person who is rendering a service.

Lest anyone might think I am defending fraudulent practices by mediums, let me inject here that I do not, in any way, approve the introduction of dishonesty in action by a psychic any more than I would approve a lack of integrity in the operation of any business or profession. It is my contention, however, that the existence of unscrupulous practitioners in this field is no indication that legitimate ones do not exist, any more than a number of unpleasant experiences with shady or unethical salesmen, lawyers, doctors, shopkeepers or mechanics makes me put them all in the category of charlatan or fake. As Professor William James said, "It only takes one white crow to prove that all crows are not black." There are *many* fine mediums or psychics.

WHAT PSYCHICS HAVE IN COMMON

In attempting to analyze the make-up of highly sensitive psychics we find that the only obvious thing they have in common is their sensitivity. Educational background runs the gamut from none at all to college degrees of the highest order. Personality varies from sullen, melancholy introverts to cheerful, dynamic extroverts. Spirituality may or may not be there; some are earthy and passional, others are almost fanatically religious or ethereally virtuous. Diet is a very strictly observed regimen with some and completely unimportant to others. Some are strong, vital and energetic, while others are frail, dull and listless. Some are grossly overweight, and others are almost emaciated. Not all, of course, are in the extreme classifications. Since most are what we consider normal, or average, people, there is no reason to assume that freakishness or abnormality is necessary, and wherever it does exist it seems to be coincidental. Some public mediums perhaps assume colorful attitudes or ways of life for purely personal reasons; trappings and picturesque atmosphere not really necessary but possibly serving as mood-setters or stage-dressings for audience appreciation.

PSYCHICS VIEWED AS SPIRITUALISTS

Spiritualists, both those who are affiliated with churches advocating the cause of honest mediumship and those who are believers in mediumistic abilities but who maintain their active membership in more traditional churches, feel that mediumship is a mixed blessing, viewed objectively and seen as a whole picture. Being so sensitive to all vibrations has distinct disadvantages, particularly if the medium does not understand the basic rules for living with a gift. Many psychics have been wrecked mentally and physically by lack of knowledge of what this sensitivity is and failure to control it. Too often more time is devoted to demonstrations and blind use of such faculties than to a serious effort to understand it and develop it properly. It is unfortunate that, particularly among the lesser known psychics, jealousy and secretiveness is more prevalent than a desire to be helpful and constructive by working together.

It is no doubt because of this antagonism among themselves that the programs of psychical research have failed to produce satisfactory results—shortsightedness has allowed standards and tests to be set by scientists who take a more or less unsympathetic attitude unless they have had some psychic experience of their own. It makes no more sense to have a research program set up to pass judgment on a psychic's ability to produce evidence to be evaluated by psychiatrists, than it would to have those same psychiatrists pass opinion on the dexterity and efficiency of a surgical specialist. They are simply too limited in their understanding of a highly specialized activity.

From the spiritualist angle, each medium is under the control and care of his own particular spirit guides. There are many of these guides influencing each person living, according to some mediums. There are Doctor Guides, Happiness Guides, Protective Guides, Earthly Guides, Financial Guides, and Spiritual Guides, to name a few. Each of these guides has his own area of influence and responsibility, and is supposed to guide us each time we are in need of, and ask for, help in his particular area of operation. Mediums, being more sensitive to these impressions and influences around us, are able to translate into oral messages those attempts to assist the less sensitive. In theory, a medium who does not have high principles attracts only those guides of questionable veracity and wisdom. Again we see evidence of the natural attraction of like for like—if, indeed, spirit contact is the activating power behind mediumistic activities.

FRAUDULENT MENTAL AND PHYSICAL MEDIUMSHIP

Mental mediumship is considered to be less productive of de-liberate fraud than the physical by some investigators. Some experienced researchers feel that, whereas some mental mediums may be fraudulent, there is more likelihood that the fraud may be uncon-scious because of dissociation and a sincere belief in the supernatu-ral nature of the impressions or control. Certainly the most flagrant deceptions exposed have been in physical forms of mediumship, showing use of hidden wires, objects secreted on or near the medium, sleight of hand, "ectoplasm" by the yard, etc.

BEGINNINGS OF PSYCHIC SENSITIVITY

It does not seem possible that there is a person alive, if he is mentally capable of understanding the meaning of the word "psy-chic," who could reasonably argue that not everyone has *some* psychic capacity. Emotional reaction to music is certainly a mind or soul experience. The troubled feeling that is sensed without words being spoken by a husband or wife when his partner is disturbed is a frequent occurrence. Deception is often sensed, seemingly without cause. Visitors can often immediately feel tension in a home where an argument has taken place earlier, even though all external evidences of such dissension are concealed. If you will think about these impressions which occur daily, you will probably agree that psychism is a part of almost everyone's nature.

To intensify and refine psychic power or ability requires practice and intelligence. Although ESP is generally accepted as meaning Extra Sensory Perception, it might also be explained as Extended Sense Perception. For example, most "normal" people see color with the physical eyes. By practice and thought, one can go beyond this and "feel" color, even if he cannot see it. By looking for auras one can develop the ability to see beyond the normally visible spectrum, seeing into the higher octaves of color. By being still and "listening" *before* you answer your telephone when it rings, it is quite possible to know who is calling before you pick up the receiver. By leaving the mind quiescent when handling a letter before it is opened, or almost any other object, it is possible to know much about the writer, owner or previous owners through the inflow of impressions.

The degree to which one develops the extension of physical senses depends upon patience and the belief in the ability to do so. Music is always the potential of a good piano; even a totally untrained finger can prove the musical tones are there. The more time, love and patience one puts into learning to play the piano, the more harmonious and easy-flowing the music becomes. Some people produce more beautiful and perfectly executed music than others, but anyone can produce a recognizable and pleasing melody if he makes a sincere effort to do so. The instrument remains mute until it is touched, and so it is with our senses. The more we try, the more we produce. A good pianist is one who practices, feels and believes in his ability to produce beautiful music; a good psychic is one who practices, feels and believes in his ability to produce evidences of his perceptive powers. A good pianist is not one who merely reads books of techniques or objectively studies written notes of beautiful music; he must be subjective enough to touch the keys. So must each man strike his own sensory keys, then with practice he can experience notable improvement in sensitivity and may finally attain a high degree of expression.

Those who do not believe in the theory that psychism can be developed in varying degrees by everyone will no doubt be amused by any suggestion that they try it. However, the only way they can prove that THEY are right (in not believing) is to try every exercise recommended—conscientiously and with an open mind of course.

TRANSITION FROM ESP TO PSYCHISM

Our extrasensory abilities are functioning subtly every day, so subtly, as a matter of fact, that we accept them as a part of our ordinary five physical senses. It is only by intensifying the functions with practice that we recognize the difference and its potential.

To carry the intensification or sensitivity into the area of medium-ship is not so easy, or, in my opinion, necessarily desirable. The history of mediumship is fraught with tragedy, misfortune, frustra-tion and ill-health. Unless one is emotionally stable and intellec-tually prepared through proper training and self-discipline, disaster could be the result. This is not to say that communion with God through proper meditation is dangerous—on the contrary, this is a wondrous experience, but contacting Spirit and contacting the spirits are considerably different.

Researchers and scientists have for many years been baffled by phenomena of various kinds because of the non-physical nature of many demonstrations. Personal participation with a mental attitude of expectation of worthwhile results, a willingness to be shown that is both free from hostility, yet equally free from blind gullibility, seems to be necessary in any successful experiment. Persons steeped in the teachings of physical sciences only in rare instances can accept, or even consider, non-physical evidence. It is true that there are men of science who have felt that psychism has much to offer, but comparatively speaking, materialistic concepts by far predomi-nate, although the past 20 years or so have lessened the proportional difference somewhat. Physical science has contributed much to our way of life insofar as its physical conduct is concerned, but the surface has just been scratched on the mental and spiritual level, scientifically speaking.

PSYCHISM CAN BE SELF-TAUGHT

This is surprising since physical sciences are costly to learn, involving extensive college training, expensive equipment, and ex-periments costly in materials and time. I do not mean to imply that this area of exploration and development is not necessary and desirable; that would be folly. But in the area of psychic science, each man has latent within him all of the abilities, material and equipment he needs to do his own researching. It is true that many are not endowed with sufficient patience and objectivity to conduct their own research in a way that would contribute much that would be considered scientifically valuable, but much of inestimable worth can be discovered by the sincere layman who is willing to take a little time each day to investigate his own ESP potential.

Learning to interpret accurately and accept without rationalization from his own experience the message or information which is picked up by the deeper consciousness and transmitted into the conscious mind is the most difficult part to master. Once this has been controlled every man can be his own proving ground.

Each recognized science has undergone growing pains. Pioneers in each field of endeavor have had to face skepticism, ridicule and even revilement in some cases. The growing recognition of parapsychology as a valid study has broken the ice and given the beginnings of the aura of respectability the study and practice of psychism deserve. Perhaps time and effort will do as much for the even more vilified field of mediumship, which is alluded to in some of our oldest and most sacred writings.

Growth of interest in psychism and mediumship

Examples of psychic or mediumistic phenomena are appearing more and more in newspapers and magazines, not to mention an increase in the number of books devoted entirely to this type of subject matter. Many books have excellent instructions for developing greater sensitivity; perhaps the simplest and best in currently popular reading is in Arthur Ford's book, *Nothing So Strange*. An older book, but one which is excellent and gives specific directions for various kinds of specialized development (such as psychometry, clairvoyance, automatism, etc.), is Hereward Carrington's *Your Psychic Powers and How to Develop Them*.

In developing psychic abilities it seems safe to say that an attitude of deep respect for these faculties is absolutely necessary. Real desire of accomplishment and a confidence in the ability to succeed are also vital. Once you begin to practice, allow yourself a reasonable time to achieve the desired results. Remember, expert athletes slowly build their prowess to a peak by developing *muscular* power and control, and you must slowly build this *mental* power and control.

In practicing or strengthening psychic abilities, it is advisable in the beginning not to sit for more than 20 minutes to a half hour for a time—if you are doing it without supervision. As is true of any transformation from the novice state to that of a polished performer, the careful and gradual building of adeptness is safer and longer lasting since fatigue and lack of real understanding usually result from "cramming."

DIFFERENCE BETWEEN THOUGHT AND IMPRESSION

While sitting, you must learn to differentiate between thought and impression. The best way to describe the feeling of thought is to say that it seems to come from inside the head while impression seems to come from the outside. The line between thought and impression is very fine; for example, in impression the emotional and intellectual reaction to something perceived is not necessarily the one you would experience if you were thinking, particularly if what you are sensing applies to someone else.

To explain more fully, let us suppose you receive an impression of a burning building. In your own experience you may never have had the misfortune of personal involvement in a tragedy of this sort, although you may have been a spectator. If the person from whom you are receiving the impression had suffered an experience of horror, loss or injury during, or as a result of, such a fire, you would feel a violent emotional response to the impression. This is not imagination; it is sensitivity. On the other hand, an elaboration or exaggeration of an impression is imagination or an intrusion of self. Learn to give clear, uncolored statements of the simple details as received. Details will not only improve in clarity with practice, but they will also increase in number and become more easily recognizable as to origination—extra sensory or rationalization.

BASIC MENTAL DISCIPLINE NEEDED

Mind discipline is a great asset in every area of life regardless of age, occupation or cultural background, whether it is used in study, work or play. Exercises to expand the power of concentration are a great help in developing sensitivity. Since these impressions are picked up by a higher level of awareness than that in which the conscious mind usually functions, we must learn to protect this higher level of awareness from external distractions. This is not to imply that one must attain freedom from consciousness or any kind of trance state—it simply means that one must learn to focus the attention in such a way that diversion of attention is cut to a minimum.

In my experience, the best and most convenient way to develop control of attention is to concentrate the thoughts on something we automatically do. For instance, in dressing ourselves, once we have decided on what to wear we dismiss the process pretty well from our minds, carrying out all manner of activities automatically while thinking about many matters not even remotely connected with the act of dressing. Instead of doing this, practice thinking of nothing but your shoes while you are putting them on—think of nothing which does not in some way pertain to those particular shoes. While brushing your teeth, close out all thoughts which are not directly related to your teeth, toothbrush or toothpaste. When combing your hair, think only thoughts about hair and the care of it. If your mind wanders, bring it back to where you want it to stay, just as you would make a naughty or adventurous child come back to his own yard if that is where he had been told to stay.

This is developing real mind control, since the habit of not concentrating on the familiar is very common. It is not too difficult to become engrossed in the novel or unfamiliar, so the real progress in discipline is made when more effort must be spent to keep the attention on the commonplace. Even one minute of true concentration is a wonderful achievement for the average person. By practicing five minutes a day during the everyday routine of getting dressed, anyone can increase this amazing power quickly and immeasurably.

Other ways to psychic and mediumship effectiveness

There are other very effective ways to extend control of attention. During a very interesting discussion of the mind and its potential with a successful businessman and philanthropist in New Orleans a few years ago, this gentleman told me that the most amazingly efficient and brilliant man he had ever met attributed his success to mind control. He had developed this control by spending five minutes each morning on total concentration on one object on his breakfast table. One morning he would select a lump of sugar and try to recall everything he ever knew about sugar. Another morning he would mentally analyze his coffee, the china, silver, or any other article he chose, excluding every thought not related to the object of his attention. This is very good if solitary meals are the individual's custom, but I doubt seriously if it would be a popular undertaking at a family table unless all were participating in the exercise.

Another good way to achieve concentration is to mentally paint a picture, carefully stroking in all details down to the most minute lines, color variations and proportions.

Emotional control necessary

Emotional control is also a very important consideration in building toward the sensitivity of psychism or mediumship. Many people are capable of almost perfect concentration but perceive only the obvious or physical attributes of that upon which they are concentrating—one must sense something beyond the obvious by reaching outside himself, so to speak. It is not a matter of will power, but more nearly like controlled drifting—controlled in that steering is put to use when necessary to assure right direction, and drifting in that force or drive is kept at a minimum. Psychic experiences are more of an emotional nature than physical, although they may result in some physical manifestation or reaction, such as with inspirational writing, painting, composing or invention, or to a greater degree in physical mediumship as in materialization, psychokinesis, apports, etc.

IMPORTANCE OF MENTAL ATTITUDE

Once again, let me repeat something which I feel cannot be overemphasized: be sure that the mental attitude is expectant of good. Even though all people interested in psychical phenomena are not religionists, almost everyone who is well versed in the subject agrees that thoughts are things and like attracts like. Spiritually minded people protect themselves with a prayer or a prayerful attitude; the more worldly mind uses a positive approach which is really a form of prayer although it is not so labeled. It is my contention that any display of calm confidence is a demonstration of a belief in good, while fear is simply faith in the wrong outcome; both are informal expressions of belief in specific eventualities.

PHYSICAL EQUIPMENT REQUIREMENTS

Although there seems to be dissension as to lighting, regularity, number of sitters or fellow-experimenters, consistency in reproducing exact conditions each time, etc., they are not so important in the elementary stages as they may be as one progresses. Very interesting results can be obtained in well-lighted rooms, with strangers, at odd moments, with or without the use of tools (such as crystal balls, Ouija boards, tables for tilting, pencil and paper for automatism, etc.). Certainly thought transference, psychometry, psychokinesis and similar abilities do not require darkness, nor do they require exact time schedules for practice. Not only are these demonstrable under differing conditions; so are some of the more mediumistic manifestations.

Some of the finest mediums I have ever seen have told me that they consider physical and mental ease most important to develop. Subdued light makes subtle "spirit lights" more readily seen, and for this reason it would be sensible to observe this condition if that is the sort of thing one wants to attain. One, if working alone or without a teacher in a group, should follow directions set forth by someone who has proven a method for himself, but, just as no two people are physically identical, so are no two alike mentally and emotionally. Within the framework of common sense, fit the methods to your own personality.

A GENERAL WARNING

Signs of developing mediumship are sometimes upsetting or disagreeable—such as dizziness, buzzing in the ears, numbness, profuse perspiration, labored breathing, unusual sounds or "touches," or a feeling of loss of consciousness. It is best to discontinue working alone if these signs occur, or even discontinue the practice entirely, unless mental and emotional stability are such that the manifestations do not become a menace to health and happiness. It is your responsibility to see that a gift does not become a threat to well-being.

SUMMARY OF CHAPTER TWO

1. All mediums are psychic, but not all psychics are mediums.
2. Mediumship and psychism fall into two categories: mental and physical.
3. A serious attitude, strongly positive and of good intent, is a must for producing the finest mediumship.
4. A good medium is entitled to a fair fee for his services.
5. Even the finest mediums are not infallible.
6. The only thing all mediums and psychics seem to have in common is sensitivity.
7. Spiritualists and scientists have differing explanations for sources of information of "messages."
8. Everyone has psychic ability which can be increased with practice.
9. You may strengthen your psychic abilities by following some simple rules included in this chapter.

THREE

The Wide World
of Seances

In the broad sense of the word "seance," one may include tea-leaf reading, card reading, Ouija-board sessions, table tilting, automatic writing experiments, or any other form of contact with the unknown or paranormal. I have even read material which referred to psychiatric analysis conferences as seances. When they think of a seance, most people picture a dark room, an eerie atmosphere, and a circle of sitters under the guidance of a modern Witch of Endor.

SEANCE EXPERIENCES

In the liberal sense of the word, I attended many seances in my years of interest in the occult, but here are some of a "limited" nature I would like to introduce first.

Tea-leaf reading

My first experience with any kind of "reader" occurred in my 20th year. I was visiting some relatives in the north that summer and at the suggestion of a cousin about my own age, I joined her for luncheon at a tea-room that featured a tea-leaf reader. I did not know how the woman operated, but she was sensational! She told me some things that I already knew, but she also told me some things I did not know since they pertained to future events or, more strictly speaking, were situations already manifest but not yet in the scope of my knowledge.

39

She told me, for example, that I would receive a letter from my father with news that my mother was ill and unable to write. The next day I received a call from the aunt to whose home all of my mail went. She told me there was a letter there from my father. When I picked up the letter later that day it informed me that my mother had unexpectedly become ill and was unable to write.

This "reader" told me a number of other things which were equally accurate, and she was just as good with my cousin.

This experience so intrigued me that I persuaded one of my aunts to go to another reader with me the next week; this was to be my aunt's first such adventure.

Both of the tea-rooms where these women worked were lovely places, not gaudy or questionable "holes-in-the-wall," but charming enough to suit the most discriminating taste. Both readers were women well past middle age, nicely dressed and obviously due complete courtesy and respect. The second reader was as good as the first and impressed both my aunt and me with her ability.

Here again I received information about events of which I had no knowledge at the time, as did my aunt. The example I have chosen to include to illustrate the accuracy of this reader concerned my aunt and uncle.

When tea-leaves are read, the person for whom the reading is being done is told to make a wish—the outcome is shown in the cup. This wish was detailed in such amazing particulars that it was the topic of discussion for many months following.

My aunt wished (silently) that my uncle would close a very important business transaction he had been working on for some time. The reader said that it would appear that her wish had come true that very evening; then word would be received by that week-end that the wish was not going to be granted, after all; but the following Monday word would be received that the wish would definitely and finally come true.

That night my uncle came home delighted because he had at last closed this important transaction; on Friday evening he came home disappointed and discouraged—he had been notified that the company with whom he had been negotiating had cancelled the orders; they wanted delivery sooner than his company could make it. On Monday he received a telegram stating that since no other concern could fill the order any sooner than his, he could consider the order valid!

In these two readings there were too many details to record here, but these examples should be sufficient to illustrate why I am open-minded when anyone mentions tea-leaf readers. No doubt these two women were developed psychics who merely used the tea leaves as focal points, although I have seen symbols clearly formed by tea leaves at such sessions.

One of the most startling of these symbols was shaped in a tea-cup during a meal I had at a local Chinese restaurant with four friends. We all worked together and, since we had to work late one night, we agreed to dine together at this particular place which featured a tea-leaf reader.

One of the women in our group was outspoken about her skepticism before we left our shop to go to the restaurant. We all agreed before we started out that after we entered the dining room we would talk only generalities in order that we would give out no information which might be helpful in the event our skeptical friend thought eaves-droppers might be lurking in the palms listening for tidbits of information to pass along to the reader.

For the benefit of anyone not familiar with the procedure involved in tea-leaf reading, let me say here that the reader does not touch the cup prior to picking it up to begin the reading. The subject drinks the tea, turns the cup upside down on the saucer to drain, and the reader only has contact with the cup after it has drained and the pattern formed by the leaves has been set without human interference or arrangement.

When the reader picked up the cup of our skeptic, she looked at it and said, "I cannot read for you. You would not believe a word I said." She turned the cup for all of us to see and there, arranged in perfect order down the inside of the cup, was a question mark about an inch and a half long! Not a leaf in any other part of the cup! How to explain this? I do not know; all I do know is that it happened.

The rest of us had good results, but the most convincing incident of the whole evening was the cup with the clear sign of the skeptic.

Coffee-ground reading

My only experience with having coffee grounds read was a more recent one. I had never heard of this method of having the future reveal itself.

I was a guest for dinner at the home of a friend, and the only other guest was a dear friend of the hostess about whom I had heard wonderful reports of psychic abilities. After dinner I was amazed to hear our hostess ask that several spoonfuls of coffee grounds be added to her few remaining swallows of demi-tasse. If there are many things less pleasant than grounds in coffee it would be difficult to name them; but I hastily asked for some, too, when I was told that I could have a reading from the grounds if I cared to do so.

The procedure was the same as with tea-leaf reading so far as turning the cup for it to drain and so on. However, in the actual reading of the cup the way this lady did it, there is no reading of the past; it is all present and future.

When the cup was turned right side up, the grounds were neatly arranged in tiny but distinct symbols, including perfectly formed letters and numbers.

The reader, a woman whom I have had the pleasure of knowing better since that night, kindly explained something of the process of reading coffee grounds. It is an old Irish custom, she said.

Starting from the handle of the cup, the inside is divided into quarters from right to left. Each quarter represents three months, the quarter first to the right of the handle being the current three month period, the second quarter the next three, and so on around the whole area. The bottom of the cup is the immediate present.

It was most interesting. The grounds showed that the most active period would take place about seven months from the reading, and the few symbols at the bottom were pertinent to my activities of that time. There was nothing vague or indefinite about the reading; it was in much detail, but mostly concentrated in a string right down one portion of time.

Card reading

I have had my cards read a few times. My first experience with this form of divining accurately foretold a sad but rather universal adventure—disappointment in love.

I had attended a church social with a friend of my brother—a spur of the moment "date" for both of us. I was not a member of this particular church and was practically unknown to anyone there save for the family of the young man who took me. The social hall where the bazaar was held had been decorated and arranged in booths featuring various "attractions," such as bakery sales, dart games, white elephant sales, etc. One of the booths was marked with a sign "Fortune Teller."

This sign drew my attention, of course, although I had an idea that, since this was an orthodox church, I would find one of those stunts where I might be asked if I wanted my palm "read" for a quarter, and upon saying "yes" would have a streak of red ink daubed in the center of my hand.

Even when I sat down at the table, which was covered with a black cloth and had on it a crystal ball and a smoking incense burner, I still did not think this was authentic. The setting was appropriate; the woman's expression was sober and intent as she greeted me across the table—she was even lightly veiled to add to the air of mysticism. I still thought it was whimsy because I was well aware of the traditionalism and orthodoxy of this particular church.

In all seriousness the woman asked me if I wanted to ask her three questions or if I wanted her to tell me three things. I chose the latter.

She picked up a deck of cards and started. When the preliminaries were over she had three piles of cards in front of her. She explained that one pile was the past, one the present and the third was the future. I do not recall what she said of the past or the present, but I know that they were accurate enough to make me realize that this was no foolish stunt. The future was the part of the reading that I never forgot.

She told me that within four days I would receive news that would break my heart and cause me to shed many tears. She said that my grief would leave as suddenly as it came, but it would be a heartache of seven months' duration.

This was absolutely true. On the fourth day after the reading I received a letter from my current heart interest, telling me that he had met and immediately married someone else! This can be rather shattering to someone as serious-minded as I was. In the seventh month following this calamity I accidently ran into this man and his wife one evening—and the spell was broken. The instant I saw him I felt nothing more than a tremendous relief that I was not the woman walking beside him. The prediction was true to the last detail!

MY FIRST REAL SEANCE

If I live to be 126 years old I will never forget my first real seance. I was never so shaken in my life, and the seance was unfortunately "staged."

It occurred when three friends and I went on a trip of several hundred miles to visit a spiritualist camp during their off-season. In spite of all my psychic study and contacts, this was to provide me my first opportunity to attend a real seance with all the trimmings.

Trumpet seance

After arriving at the camp we made inquiries about where we might find someone who would hold a trumpet seance for us. For the benefit of those who do not know what a trumpet seance is, I will briefly explain it here.

A trumpet is a light aluminum instrument, shaped like a megaphone, usually collapsible, variable in length from about twelve inches to three feet, and often trimmed with luminous paint which makes it visible in the darkness of a seance room. This trumpet is used to amplify "spirit voices" and can be levitated and moved about with no visible means of support or locomotion.

We were directed to the home of a gentleman who we were told had retired but might possibly be persuaded to give us a trumpet demonstration. When we arrived he gave us a cordial reception, served us tea and was the soul of kindness, but did not give us any encouragment in our interest in trumpet work.

After an hour or so of persuasion and pleading on our part, the poor old fellow finally weakened. He told us that if we would return to his house that evening he would do his best for us, although he cautioned us that he was out of practice since he had retired some years earlier. He promised us nothing but his best efforts, since we had come so many miles in such great hopes.

At the appointed hour we returned to the old gentleman's home. His house was, I believe he said, 75 years old. It looked every minute of it, and although it was clean and neat inside, it was so musty and airless that we felt the windows had never been open once during the whole 75 years.

We were ushered into a tiny room off a short hall which led from the living room to a side entrance. This room, about eight by ten feet, was completely sealed from both air and light except for the door through which we entered. A bare bulb which hung from the ceiling provided the only illumination and revealed straight chairs lined up against one wall and a wicker chair and sofa against the opposite wall. At one end of the room stood a table and the opposite wall was the one which contained the door through which we had entered, and which was now closed.

We four were instructed to sit in the straight chairs, and the medium sat on the wicker sofa opposite us. Before he turned out the light he showed us his two trumpets with luminous bands and explained what we were to expect if he succeeded in his attempt to raise them and produce spirit voices.

I was seated in the chair farthest from the door; the other sitters were at my right. After a few minutes of self-conscious singing which the old gentleman had said would raise the vibrations, we sat quietly waiting for something to happen.

Never will I forget the feeling of horror that flooded over me when something *did* happen!

There was a weird skittering sound across the floor right at my feet, and I was paralyzed by the sound of raspy breathing and the sight of the luminous circle around one of the trumpets suspended at face level between the friend on my right and me. To add to my panic, the friend on my right grabbed my leg in her excitement and I didn't know *what* had me!

Those first few moments of that seance were the most terrifying of my whole life, I am sure.

Then came a voice from the trumpet which by then had drifted to the other end of the line of sitters. A hoarse whisper said, "Be patient."

Relief came with that sound; I knew it was the old man's voice, and somehow this was comforting. I was still suffering acutely from suffocation, but at least the panic was gone.

Although the trumpet passed in front of me several times and various voices came through it, it never again stopped near me nor was I ever addressed directly. The others maintained a running conversation with the voices, but I sat desperately longing for some fresh air.

Because I was so quiet the friend at the other end of the line spoke up and asked me if I were all right. I replied that I was, but felt that I just *had* to have some air. She asked the medium if we could have the door to the dark hallway open in order to give some ventilation. He said he thought it would be all right, and opened it himself.

The door to the living room at the end of the hall was shut, but from under a crack at the bottom a faint trace of light from a lamp in the room seeped out into the hall. This tiny bit of light, although almost imperceptible, was sufficient to make the now open doorway of the room in which we were sitting faintly discernible in the terrible blackness. Against this dim difference, because of the position in which I sat, I could see no movement, nor could the sitter at the other end of the line. But the two women in the middle could see the movements made by the old gentleman. He moved all about the room, even stood on the chair on his side of the narrow room. Using first one trumpet and then the other, he waved them all about in various directions and at different levels.

How the seance was staged

Since he handled only one trumpet at a time, there was always one trumpet standing on the floor. The two sitters in the middle decided to join in the game and they took turns with the alternate trumpet, passing it back and forth between themselves. Each time the old fellow put down his trumpet they would put theirs down and pick up his. From the remarks that came through from that time on it was obvious that the poor old fellow was completely baffled by this turn of events.

It was a shameful thing to do in a way because the poor soul had tried desperately to discourage us from the beginning. I am sure that his only intent was to make a sincere effort to satisfy us. Nonetheless, this is the way the last half of that particular seance was conducted.

UNNERVING EXPERIENCES DURING A SEANCE

Since this first memorable seance I have attended a number of others. The feeling of uneasiness has gradually left so that by now I am completely comfortable during any manifestations—with two exceptions. I become nauseated in the course of a seance conducted by a sham medium, and I loathe having chiffon or gauze draperies dragged about my person and clammy artificial hands touch me during these fake demonstrations. Even the sound of pretended spirit voices upsets me. I suppose that my rage at the insult to my intelligence is the real cause of my physical distress.

Apports

The only other time I have ever become completely unnerved during a seance was during an apport demonstration. An apport is an object which apparently drops from nowhere, a gift from a discarnate entity—a flower, a gem, a meaningful relic, or almost anything one could imagine. Some of them disappear as inexplicably as they come, and others last as long as any ordinary similar object normally would.

Some apports are valuable and others have no intrinsic value. One of my aunts received a valuable amethyst in this manner. The jeweler who mounted it for her remarked about its unusual cut and beauty. This from a sitting she paid three dollars to attend!

I once attended one particular apport demonstration with five other sitters. I was told by a voice speaking directly to me (once again in absolute darkness) that if I would hold my hands cupped out in front of me an effort would be made to apport something to me. I no sooner put my hands in the required position when I thought I would faint dead away—the voice announced that I was to be given a "head"! I had momentary visions of a shrunken head being dropped into my outstretched hands.

Fortunately, almost with the words, I felt a little stone-like object drop into my palm. I have rarely experienced such tremendous relief.

Materialization seances

A materialization seance—one during which spirits assume visible form—is something I resisted attending for a long time. I was not exactly frightened by the thought—it was more a feeling of revulsion which made me reluctant. I even passed up an opportunity to sit in on a materialization demonstration with one of the greatest materialization mediums then living. A group of friends went and they returned from this session filled with enthusiasm.

I resisted all attempts to persuade me to attend others until fairly recently. I have not as yet formed a conclusion about this experience, so I will not go into detail about it. People far more familiar with this phase of mediumship than I have seen many and have definite opinions, which they have expressed. At least I have wet my feet, so to speak, so the worst is over.

My experience in sitting in "circles" in my own home or in those of friends, with no professional medium present, has been interesting. To be sure, we have had no earth-shaking results, but we did have some unusual manifestations. We proceeded carefully and studiously. We had the satisfaction of knowing that whatever *did* transpire was really genuine and not the result of any hanky-panky on the part of mercenary or self-seeking frauds. We accomplished enough to know that many inexplicable things will occur if the sitters will exercise patience, understanding and intelligence. We didn't have to worry about jokers or thrill-seekers. Boredom eliminated the latter and our own experience took care of the former.

DISCOUNTING PSYCHIC PHENOMENA

It is difficult to discount psychic phenomena when one reads some of the eminent names in the field of serious investigation—well-known authors, lecturers, scientists, theologians, and so on. A good book, a lecture sponsored by a well-known civic group, and experiences recounted from the pulpit of a recognized church by an ordained minister can be powerful persuaders. To hear a medium relay messages containing names and details of great significance to someone he has never before seen is also convincing. But even harder to discredit is the evidence of your own eyes and ears when these things happen in your own study group made up of your own trusted friends.

Despite the fact that I have heard much, read much and had many readings myself, I still feel profound pleasure from hearing a stranger tell me things over a tea-cup, a pile of cards, from a platform in a church, or in a private reading or circle.

It piques my curiosity to be a part of such a little understood phenomenon and stimulates my mind to be a part of the investigation of the undeveloped potential of man. How can I explain the ability of a total stranger to pick me out of a roomful of a hundred persons or so, call me by name and tell me of something of great significance to me? If it is telepathic—a conclusion which may be drawn if I have knowledge of the information given—it is still a wonderful ability. If it is precognition—an inference which is valid if *no one* had any way of knowing the facts revealed because they had bearing on an event yet to transpire—the challenge is even greater, especially if time proves the prediction to be accurate.

Whether these things happen because man has mental resources as yet undeveloped to the fullest or because discarnate entities give the data, the fact that they do happen is enough of a stimulus to spur me on to attempt to discover and understand the "why and how" of it.

CAN TELEPATHY BE THE ANSWER TO PSYCHIC COMMUNICATION?

I remember one of my early meetings with a very fine medium. I had absolutely no idea of a connection with the spirit she described to me as one who had come into her home with me. I could place no one who fitted the description she gave of a physical condition which preceded the attack which took his life. It was not until the next day when I told the details of this reading to another member of my family that all of the pieces fell into place.

How could this have been telepathy? I had absolutely no knowledge of the facts. They were certainly not once known but forgotten, for the death had been too recent for that to have been the case. No one else in the room even knew the man of whom she spoke. The glib explanations one hears of such things in an effort to minimize them are suspiciously like the early expoundings by "experts" about why the earth cannot be round, man cannot fly, automobiles would never replace horses, etc.

An interesting experiment with mediums

There is one interesting experiment I try any time I am in the presence of a medium. I do not do this with the intention of setting a trap; if that were my intention I would fabricate someone upon whom to concentrate.

I have some relatives by marriage who are members of a spiritualist church. This religious faith has been of great comfort to them and because of my knowledge of their experiences and belief, my respect for this religious concept is extensive. Also in the family, this a blood relationship, was an aunt who passed away some years ago. There has never been a medium mention this aunt to me or to the members of the family who are spiritualists.

Each time I go to a seance it is this particular aunt upon whom I concentrate. I have conditioned myself to think of her in an expectant way so my thoughts will not be colored by the negative attitude that she will not be mentioned because of past failures. I think of no one but her, generally, and have never yet had a medium mention her name. Why? If telepathy is the answer to how other information is gleaned by a reader, why is it that this name which I keep foremost in my thoughts has not been forthcoming?

The nearest thing to reference to her has been an explanation given to other family members that sometimes many years pass before a spirit is interested in, or capable of, communication. This is not unreasonable, and I can accept it as an explanation of why there has never been a contact from this particular person. After all, we don't write letters to our family members who are away as often as we might or even should.

Why is it that some names come through with such ease and frequency, along with some that have no significance or readily recognizable connection? How about the really unusual names?

One of my grandmothers had a most unusual first name. This name has been given to me twice in public messages during church services, an experience which startled me because the name is so unusual that I never expect to hear it given properly. I rarely think of her as a possible communicant, not only because of the difficult name but because my grandmother was not a believer in communication after death. How can one account for the fact that her name has come through to me when I was not thinking of her? What part of our consciousness is being read if it is not really spirit contact? Above all, no matter what it is, HOW IS IT DONE?

A PSYCHIC EXPERIENCE WITH ARTHUR FORD

One Sunday evening I attended a church service in a city about 75 miles away from home. Three friends and I decided to attend on the spur of the moment. It was a church none of us had attended previously.

When we arrived at the little church we were delighted to find that Arthur Ford, one of the world's great mediums, was substituting as minister for that particular service. Here was a man of whom I had read and heard a great deal, but I had never had the opportunity to see him work. Needless to say, he had never heard of me.

Mr. Ford, at the conclusion of a fine sermon, announced that he would do a short portion of the message service, the balance of which would be done by one of the regular church workers. This was really a privilege—to think we were to see one of the most famous men in the world of spirit communication in action!

I was stunned when mine was one of the first names he called to receive a message. There was absolutely no groping or hesitation— he not only enunciated my name clearly, he looked at me as he did so. In the congregation of approximately 120 people, some of whom he knew, there was no mistaking that he was addressing me.

He made some accurate remarks about my personal life and then went on to say that the message he had was one I was to relay to someone else in my family. I did not recognize the name of the person with whom the message was concerned, nor did I recognize the name of the deceased person to whom the message was attributed. Mr. Ford again stated that this message was not for me personally but was to be passed along to a relative of mine.

As I had been instructed to do, I passed along the information the next day. I was not at all surprised to find that the names and the meaning of the communication were most significant to the person to whom I relayed them.

In another visit to this church my daughter went with me, and this was to be my daughter's first time to see a psychic at work. Interestingly, she was chosen to receive a message. It was particularly intriguing to hear this total stranger give a message about plans in which my daughter was involved at the time, hear her tell how it would appear that the plans would have to be altered, and then finish by saying that the original plans would be carried out after all. Neither of us could accept as even a remote possibility the event which she had predicted as a threat to the completion of them. It was just a matter of days, however, and she was proven to be precisely right in all details.

LEGAL BARRIERS AGAINST SPIRITUALISTIC CHURCHES

In the city where I live there is a "legal" barrier against spiritualist churches. I do not understand how this can possibly be enforced, but it is. I feel that it is a gross injustice that those people who would like to carry out their worship program in affiliation with one of these nationally recognized church organizations must, if they live in this city, seek their religious programs elsewhere.

If these churches were unacceptable everywhere in the country, I could believe that there might be some good reasoning behind such an attitude. But when other communities allow churches of this persuasion to function without prejudice within their boundaries, how can such unfair action be justified?

There are no doubt other communities with the same policy, but my own opinion is that any governmental agency which taxes and licenses religious groups out of existence in such a prejudicial manner stifles the ideal of freedom of religious worship, one of the principles upon which our country is founded.

To be sure there are many areas where reforms could be introduced within the framework of spiritualism—but is this not true of unionism, politics, and other religious bodies which come into the structure of our daily lives? To place an ordained minister in the same category as a gypsy fortune teller is a relic of a Salem witchcraft type of thinking. It is unfortunate that any part of our country is guilty of such antiquated irrationality.

In the little town immediately south of the city in which I live I attended services in a Spiritualist church for about a year. I have never seen more dedication on the part of any church group. The services were almost identical to the worship rites of any of the many orthodox churches I have attended over the years: hymns, prayers, sermons, all in the expected manner. The chief differences were that a healing service preceded the customary service, and a "message service" was the final segment. Never did I see or hear anything suggestive of commercialism, irreverence or sensationalism any more than I have seen in some of the more traditional churches.

One evening a few years ago I attended a service held in a civic building in a neighboring community. This meeting, sponsored by the small local spiritualist group in that city, was held in this large hall because it was known that this particular visiting medium would draw more people than the group's regular quarters could accommodate. The speaker, an ordained minister in one of the largest denominations in this country, had become a Spiritualist minister after he discovered that he was mediumistic.

Because of my acquaintance with the sponsoring minister, I know there was no collusion. During the message portion of the service, the minister spoke to a man sitting directly across the aisle from me. The communication, purportedly from the man's deceased father, was beautiful and reassuring. The man burst into tears as he listened to the words. I later learned that this was an important message to him and his wife. They considered it very evidential because, although the wording was obscure to all but them, it was much to the point—and moved them greatly, since his father had been a suicide. In light of this information the message made sense and it brought them release from much anxiety. I see nothing wrong with a practice which gives so much comfort to sorrowing people.

HOW MEDIUMS DEVELOP COMMUNICATION WITH RECIPIENTS

Skilled and highly developed mediums are able to so word a message that the recipient of the communication is spared any embarrassment through personal exposure and yet the meaning is perfectly clear to him. Only a few times have I ever heard a medium give a message which made someone uncomfortable or conspicuous because of the open revelation of personal matters. This does take place in private readings, but there one should expect and want frankness.

It is not unusual to be a sitter and hear denials of messages, or for that matter to deny them oneself. I recall a seance in which someone I knew very well denied the message she was given. There was no reason for the medium to generalize or give this information in obscure terms, so she spoke clearly and openly about a deceased brother of the woman she was addressing. The only thing wrong was that this woman had no such brother.

The next day when she told her mother of this experience, she was informed that she had had such a brother but he had died before she was born. This was her first knowledge of him, yet the medium knew. . . . How?

The years of study, investigation and participation have been wonderful and satisfying. Boredom is nonexistent in my life. There is no question in my mind about the value of an *intelligent* interest in the occult. The quest for hidden treasure appeals to the young in heart, and the pursuit of the treasure hidden within oneself makes the hunt much more exciting. Add to this the knowledge that once a strike is made the "vein" will never be depleted! What more could anyone ask?

SUMMARY OF CHAPTER THREE

1. Tea leaves, coffee grounds and cards can lead to convincing readings.
2. Some "fake" seances can be unnerving, humorous, and/or well motivated.
3. Telepathy may be a factor in mediums' demonstrations, but there isn't convincing proof of it.
4. In some areas there are suppressive laws against Spiritualist churches.
5. There is much practical value in an intelligent interest in the occult for daily living.

FOUR

The Reality

of Human Auras

How do you "infect" other people? Do you know that you carry with you potent contagion, resulting in either good or bad manifestations of a physical, mental or emotional nature in everyone with whom you come in contact? This chapter will show you how to control this awesome power of psychic communication for your own good as well as for others.

Each of us is responsible for the nature of the contagion we carry with us everywhere we go. There are many "plague" carriers who are completely unaware of the infection they are spreading. Fortunately, there are many others, for example, who radiate "healing" *but* are unaware of the source of the good they carry with them.

WHAT THE HUMAN AURA IS

The human aura is a fascinating and powerful field of forces, inherent in each individual, and maintained by him. Herein lies tremendous protection, great persuasion, and one of our main power lines of contact and influence with others, as well as "infection" of many positive and negative types. It operates both visibly and invisibly in shaping human experiences.

Evidences of auras universally accepted

Almost every religious work of Christian art, as well as that of other religions, regardless of the medium used, shows recognition of the presence of the aura. Crowns and headdresses worn by kings and priests are symbolic of the aura, a symbolism used from time immemorial in all known civilizations of the world. The designs contained in these are said to represent the impressions of the Akashic records supposed to be in each individual aura.

In stained glass windows and similar multi-color art forms, the hues showing in the garments worn by the subjects were generally indicative of the auric colors of the person represented, whether he was shown with a halo, or nimbus, or not.

In literature, including the Holy Bible, there are countless references to it, usually terming it a great light shining forth, or some similarly descriptive phrase. Since the brilliance is determined by spirituality, as size is determined by vitality, only the most holy persons are generally portrayed with brightly visible auras, usually about the head of the person.

Among those investigators who admit the reality of the aura there seems to be disagreement as to its nature. Some maintain that it is one mass composed of blending and intermingling colors occupying the same space; others are equally certain that it is made up of a series of layers, each with its own place and significance. There is general agreement that, with an understanding of the meaning of the colors, fluctuation and size of the aura, it is a clear record of the health, character and mood of the person from whom it is emanating. The ability to read more than this in an aura does, I believe, require more than average psychic ability.

A definition of an aura

An aura is variously described as fluidic, vibrational, subtle, invisible, vaporous, radiational, sensory and electrical. It is referred to as hypothetical, real, supposed, theoretical and sensory. Obviously, since dictionaries and encyclopediae not only contradict each other but themselves as to the specifics of the aura, it is one of the most challenging and stimulating phases of investigation for even the newest student of the "unknown"—its presence can be easily discerned, thereby providing more *immediate* material with which to work than some of the other phenomena can furnish.

According to most writers on the subject of auras, the ability to see the luminescence is an ability peculiar to clairvoyants alone. My own conclusion, after much experimentation, is that I can agree with this claim *only* if those making it are ready to admit that clairvoyance can be demonstrated by practically anyone who will take five minutes to do so. Certainly, in the *popular* sense of the word, "clairvoyant" is much too mystical a term to use for this ability—it is merely a readily developed extension of the normal eyesight.

HOW TO PROVE THE REALITY OF THE AURA

To prove the reality of the aura and the ease with which the ability to see it can be developed, why not look yourself? You may practice looking at your own in a mirror or that of someone else if anyone else is available. In the event you are looking for your own, put yourself in the position of the other person and have the mirror positioned where *you* should be according to the following directions.

Since the size of the aura is determined by the vitality of the subject, select for your first attempt someone you feel reasonably sure is healthy and energetic. Have the subject sit or stand in front of a plain non-reflective wall or similar smooth surface. Since the auric emanations are subtle, do your first aura-looking in subdued light with the subject so situated as to eliminate shadows behind him if possible. Look at the forehead just above the space between the eyebrows. Keep your gaze unmoving on this spot and, as the eyes tire and the feeling of focus begins to change to an almost unseeing stare, the aura will become visible. In the beginning, if the gaze moves from the focal point to the aura, the aura seems to fade away. However, continued practice develops the ability to see more clearly and directly so it becomes possible to observe the size, color and movement without losing sight of it. Some people find it helpful in the beginning to squint the eyes, so if at first you do not get satisfactory results try this method. Unless one has visual difficulties success should be obtained in a matter of minutes.

Appearance of the aura

The human aura appears somewhat like a luminous vapor, pulsating or gently moving, seen distinctly most often around the head and shoulders, but sometimes seen in its entirety enveloping the whole body. As one's perception of the aura becomes more developed, the colors become more clearly seen. Occasionally, rays will be seen flashing or spiralling outward, sometimes projecting beyond the outer edge of that part which is perceptible as an ovoid or egg-shaped mist. Sincerity, reverence or enthusiasm quite often produce bright active flashes—I have seen flashes so brilliant as to be almost "blinding," silver spirals and cone-like projections frequently in the auras of speakers on a lecture platform or pulpit. On one occasion I saw a bright white cross about 24 inches long projected from the left shoulder of a woman minister. I have also seen demonstrations of the deliberate change of the color of the outer edge of the aura, brought about by concentration on strong emotional states, such as anger, love, excitement, etc.

Disadvantage of involuntary aura viewing

I should like to inject here, as a purely personal viewpoint, that it is not my desire to see auras without conscious or deliberate effort. The involuntary seeing of them can be developed so that they are spontaneously and constantly visible under almost any conditions. I remember very clearly a story I heard a number of years ago when I first began my subjective study along this particular line. A lecturer, during a discussion of her experiences as a teacher of aura reading, told of some of the disadvantages of developing this ability to the point where the seeing was involuntary. One of her students was an ordained minister who, despite her warnings, developed his ability to the point that he could no longer shut out the sight of auras; he saw auras wherever he looked. The hypocrisy and negative characteristics constantly visible to him in his congregation as he delivered his sermons so disturbed him that he could no longer look at his parishioners as he addressed them. This, in turn, so upset his congregation that he began to lose their attention and respect. Finally he gave up his ministry and became a teacher in a theological school.

This story is a good illustration of a gift which became a burden when it controlled its recipient. Being in command of all psychic abilities, rather than allowing them to be in control without regard to time or circumstance, is most important. I would rather spend a moment or two in a deliberate focusing in order to see an aura whenever I have a purpose in mind, than to see them involuntarily and run the risk of unnecessary shock or disillusionment.

How to interpret auras

The accurate interpretation of the various facets of auras requires much study. The non-appearance of an aura does not always mean impending death or that the subject is an incarnation of the Devil himself, although there are some who insist that this is so. The latter thought is based upon the old teachings that the Devil could be identified by the fact that he could not, even if challenged, show his "light." Failure might be due to several factors, including poor lighting conditions, temporarily weak power of concentration or a vibrational frequency much too high for ordinary viewers to catch.

Aside from the fact that I can *see* auras, there are a number of other convincing proofs of their existence; at least, I find these satisfactory enough to include here. I recall attending a dinner where one of the other guests could show the size of anyone's aura in a way which was startling. She would place her hands, palms inward, on either side of the subject's head about 18 inches away. As she moved her hands closer to the edge of the auric field, the rest of us watched. When her hands came in contact with the outer visible edge of the radiations, there was a noticeable crackling sound which could be clearly heard anywhere in the room. This may not be an uncommon faculty, but it is the only time I have ever seen such a demonstration.

Dr. Walter J. Kilner, who was associated with St. Thomas Hospital in London, developed the Aura Screen and Aura Goggles for intensifying the visibility of the aura with the aid of these devices, and did much to validate the theories of the pioneers working in this new field of investigation. There are also numerous devices now available for the measurement of the frequency of the auric energy vibrations. Other proofs notwithstanding, there is no more satisfactory evidence than the development of one's own ability to see them.

To disprove the cries of "suggestion," "imagination," and so on, which will always enter the discussion with the novice, do this: have as many people as possible look at the aura of one person, making written notes about what each sees without consultation or comparison until all have put down details, such as color, size and shape. Allowing for slight variations which may result from semantic differences and diverse degrees of development, evaluate the results. I have been in a room with 12 people observing one aura with complete concurrence in all details.

How to build your aura

There are numerous exercises with which to build a strong aura and to maintain it. Since the size of the aura is determined by physical vitality, it goes without saying that all sensible rules of good health should be observed, such as eating nutritious food, getting adequate rest, etc. The less obvious way is through breathing exercises. These must be slowly and carefully used unless the person attempting them has been trained in the art of proper breathing. As a novice in rhythmic breathing exercises, I found the best way for me to do it without danger or discomfort was to stand by an open door or window, or out in the open air, inhale through the mouth to a slow count of eight, hold the lungs expanded for the same count, and exhale through the nostrils at the same rate of count. Immediately inhale again, and so on. Gradually increase the count a few numbers a day as you do the exercise for several minutes at a time several times a day. When you reach the point of doing the exercise without too much conscious concentration on the rhythm and can comfortably use the count of about 15, then begin the visualizing part of the process.

Picture a cylinder of light about nine feet high and about five feet in diameter, with yourself suspended in the middle. See the light as clear and bright, a white light with rays of pastels playing through it. Draw into this cylinder all of the spiritual protection you wish by thinking of it as permeated with the Christ consciousness. If you wish, you may also fill it with the sound of beautiful music, since music has great vibration-building force.

Protection through the aura

As you master the visualization part of the exercise, extend the diameter of the light surrounding you. This is undoubtedly what

Paul refers to as the "whole armor of God" in Ephesians 6:11–17. The description included in these passages fits the protection which is obtained from possessing a strong aura, and the all-encompassing parts mentioned as being important.

Materialists may deny the effectiveness of protecting oneself in this manner, but the results of the building will be visible to all with the ability to see and the protective qualities will be demonstrated in often unexpected ways. Some esoteric schools refer to the aura as "the ring-pass-not."

Not long ago there appeared in a national magazine an article which contained in it a reference to the effectiveness of this visualized circle of light in its projected form. It gave credit to this means of protection in the discouragement of neighborhood dogs approaching a small female dog whose owner had given her a circle of light by mentally projecting it. A friend of mine attributed the fact that his children did not contract any childhood diseases, even in epidemics, to the circle of light with which he kept each of them surrounded. A resident of a nearby town walked on live coals and held white hot iron in his hand without discomfort or harm, fully believing that his auric armor would protect him, and it obviously did. According to Helena Blavatsky in her book *Isis Unveiled,* there were reported to be holy men in India who would allow guns to be fired at them, secure in the belief that their auras were sufficiently strong to deflect the bullets.

Case histories of auric protection

Since my own experiences are more real to me than those of someone else, I should like to recount three of them here, briefly. Two are physical in nature and the other is more occult:

I was preparing coffee one morning in a vacuum type coffee-maker. The seal which held the top and bottom of the pot together tightly to allow the vacuum to be created was either not properly secured or was no longer as tightly fitting as it had been, for, as the boiling water bubbled up into the top, the two parts separated slightly. I picked up a towel, pressed the two parts together and stood there holding the top in place until the pot could reseal itself. When all of the water appeared to be in the top half of the pot I removed my hand and released the pressure I had been exerting. As soon as I took my hand away the whole top blew off, drenching me with boiling coffee.

As the first drop hit me, a thought flashed through my mind: "This *cannot* burn me!" The spot where the first drop hit me was scalded and later turned into a blister which left a slight mark for a while. The rest of the coffee, at least six cupfuls, thoroughly saturated me but could not have even touched my skin, because I did not find so much as heightened color anywhere on my body except where the first drop hit. I accept the auric protection as my armor against a disfiguring burn.

My second experience was of a similar nature. This time I put my hand, palm downward, into a pan of hot bacon fat. My mind rejected the thought of burning in a flash, but my reflexes were not as fast as my thought. Although the entire surface of my palm and fingers were covered with fat, there was only a tiny burn where the first contact was made. This again I can only explain as a powerful protective force present in the aura, concentrated where it was needed.

My third experience was of a considerably different nature, but the auric protection worked again for me. This episode may be difficult for many readers to believe, but I am sure enough of its acceptance by more advanced psychic students to include it here as follows.

Among my acquaintances there are many who understand and practice both mental and astral projections. As is usually the case in any field of development, there are some misguided souls who use their abilities for questionable experiments, motivated by one idea or another. One Sunday afternoon I was alone in my home and stretched out on my bed to relax before getting dressed to go out. I do not believe I had fallen into a very deep sleep state because I had looked at the clock to see how long I had to rest, and this incident took place about four minutes after I had looked at the time. I was suddenly startled out of a drowsy state by a noise which I took to be the sound of a wire shorting out—a distinct crackling—followed immediately by the acrid smell of smoke such as comes from a short circuit. I jumped off the bed and hastily checked the outlets in my room. The sharp smell was very strong, almost chokingly strong, but I could find nothing to account for it. I went into the other rooms of the house, checking all wires and outlets, when I suddenly realized that the odor of burning was only in my room. I rushed back and double-checked the wiring. Then it struck me! There was no *physical* evidence other than sound and odor because this was not a completely physical experience.

The explanation was that it probably had been attempted invasion of privacy by someone's projecting himself astrally into my presence, and the protective aura in which I encase myself had done its good work again.

I observed the people I knew who experimented in this fashion of astral projection. It soon became evident that one of the persons so experimenting in projecting himself astrally has avoided me consistently ever since, for no apparent reason deciding to discontinue what had been a fairly regular association in group discussion work. Once again the auric protection worked for me against psychic attack.

HOW AURAS AFFECT OTHER PEOPLE

How does the aura affect other people? Every first impression we give or receive is the result of the condition of our auras. What we are sending forth into the very air around us are vibrations, the nature of which we determine ourselves. If they are compatible with the type of vibration emanated from the person or persons with whom we are in contact, all will react favorably and a comfortable meeting results. If they are not of a similar frequency, disharmony follows. The difference in the rate or kind of frequency determines the degree of compatability or dissension. Here is a manifestation of the truth of a statement that like attracts like.

When we are experiencing any of the stress emotions and reacting to them by allowing negative vibrations to emanate from us, we upset the aura of everyone with whom we come in contact, even in the most casual way. Unless the person so contacted has a very strongly positive aura, we upset or disturb his vibrations, resulting in a depletion of his physical, mental or emotional being.

How weak auras draw on strong auras

A weak aura will draw on a strong aura. I once attended a lecture by the well-known Eileen Garrett. During the question and answer period which followed her address, a question was asked about auras. Before answering the query, Mrs. Garrett said that she had been observing two women sitting in the front area of the auditorium. Mrs. Garrett said that she could see that one of the women had a headache and healing was being transmitted or drawn from the other woman's aura into that of the headache sufferer. This "transfusion" was taking place without the knowledge of either woman! It is so whenever we are in the proximity of anyone; we either give or we draw. This is why we are morally responsible to understand this particular area of our relationship to others; we must keep our own auras strong so that we do not become depleted by our contacts, nor should we allow such weakness to develop in our own that we become a drain on others'.

HOW HEALTH DEPENDS ON AURAS

Paracelsus in his writings and theories accepted the aura as a reality. He believed that the emanations of man's body were impervious to disintegration but not derangement. Ill health was simply disharmony in the aura, and by reharmonizing the vibrations by contact with a very healthy body, and with a transfer of the elements present in a healthy person's aura, a state of good health could be restored to anyone who was ill.

This is why spiritual healers work in and around the aura of the people who come to them for treatment. They are trying to effect a transfusion. Some healers work by thought transference, attempting to influence the aura with mentally projected vibrations which will be absorbed by the consciousness of the patient. Others work by laying on the hands, this direct contact with the body flooding the entire being with a healing force.

Some healers who work with the laying on of hands assert that this was the secret of the healing power of Jesus, His auric emanations being so strong and so highly spiritual that they produced complete and immediate healings. In Chapter 8 of St. Luke, when He spoke of feeling that the "virtue" had gone out of Him when the woman touched the hem of His garment, does it not seem possible that He felt the drain of energy from His aura? Because the touch caught Him unaware, the energy loss was noticeable—He had not been prepared for the drain and so had not effected simultaneous replacement.

Health diagnosis by aura

Spiritual healers who diagnose illnesses do so frequently by analyzing the aura. Depressions in the outline, discoloration or breaks reveal much to them. I have seen evidences such as great gaps in the auras of cancer victims and, at the other end of the scale, small indentations indicative of slight discomfort.

There is some disagreement about the meaning of the colors associated with the study of auras—whether the facet with which one is dealing is healing, character analysis or emotional states. Generally speaking, in healing the healer concentrates on violet and its various shades for soothing, bright green for vigor, orange and yellow for upliftment in the nervous system. He uses red for stimulation and deep, clear blue for soothing the organic system and the blood. Blue is soothing and cooling, red is enriching and warming to the blood. In concluding the mental projection of color into the aura of a patient the healer generally concentrates on dazzling white, this being inspirational for both persons and restores the energy of the healer.

In reading character from the aura the following seems to be the consensus of evidence of the significance of the various colors:

Black: is very rarely seen, indicates deep malice and hatred, the ultimate negative. The greying of any color seen in the aura is a negative condition manifesting. The same is true with brown tinges. The degree of negativity is determined by the degree of darkness.

Red: if deep, indicates a sensual nature; if tinged with black or brown it indicates anger; crimson indicates love and loyalty; pink shows optimism and cheerfulness.

Blue: if deep and strong indicates a very religious nature; lighter blue represents a person with high ideals; medium blue shows great mental powers; pale blue shows great imagination and an alert and active mind. Blue is always an indication that the individual is more mental than physical, greyed off if the person is melancholy.

Green: indicates versatility or ingenuity in its clear deep shades; cunning or avarice if muddy; in its lighter bright tints it indicates healing power. Green is also the color of growth, sympathy and charity in its lighter shades, usually interpreted as indicating a compassionate nature. Grey-green shows jealousy, morbidity and envy, which explains why we use the expression "green with envy."

Yellow: is a color about which there is much disagreement; some contend that it is strictly a color of the intellect, while others maintain that it has to do with the emotional nature. All agree that it is a highly desirable color, since it is highly spiritual. It is one of the high octave colors and, in the golden shades, expresses great spiritual attainment, whether through mental processes or a sympathetic understanding of others. Negative, or greyed, yellow is the color of fear or cowardice.

Orange: shows a balance of the mental and physical, usually indicative of sociability and extroversion, with a love for people in general.

Violet: a blend of red and blue, is a very high color and only shows in highly evolved people because it comes only to those who are deeply spiritual with a great love for all humanity. Sometimes one may see lavender or violet flashes in the aura of someone at prayer or in meditation. It is rarely seen as the predominating color in auras in a materialistic workaday world.

White: transcends all other colors and, when one develops the ability to really see colors in auras, is seldom seen. Only very rarely is one privileged to be in the presence of such a person. There is most often a mother-of-pearl effect present, which is very subtle, but which renders the silvery effect—this, too, is a *very* high octave, difficult to attain.

INDICATIONS OF DEATH BY AURA

I have known of many experiences which indicate that the aura does leave the human body before death. A classic example of this type of aura indication is one attributed to an English diplomat (a psychic also), who was saved from death in an elevator crash because he noticed that the passengers already in the car had no auras visible.

A psychic friend of mine was observing auras of others in a self-service laundromat while her own washing was in a machine. She saw a woman step out of her aura, saw it dissipate, and watched the woman leave—without an aura. Some hours later she was told that the woman had died of a heart attack not too long after returning home from the laundromat.

I know a young lady who is one of the few people I have ever met who have seen auras all their lives and do not realize that everyone does not see them. She and her husband never could agree about an employee of theirs, she maintaining that the man was light, her husband insisting that he was dark. One evening she came in contact with the person in question and was startled to see that he was dark, as her husband had contended all along. A few hours later the man was dead, murdered by a hold-up man! It was not until some months later, during our discussion of auras, that she realized that the difference of opinion between her and her husband had arisen because she was basing her argument on the color of the man's aura, while her husband was seeing only the complexion of the man. Here again was an example of the aura seemingly leaving the body before death.

One's skepticism does not prevent the perception of auras, unless the skepticism is so colored with hostility that the doubter will not make a conscientious effort to see them. I remember one evening when a discussion about auras arose. There was, among those present, an Army officer who was not only skeptical but downright insulting about what he thought of anyone who would even consider such a possibility. He was loud in his rejection of "the whole idiotic thing," and typical of the sort of person who is so busy opening his mouth that he has not time to open his mind, he would not participate in the experiment. His wife, a quiet, unobtrusive woman, sat without comment and participated with interest in the test with us. Suddenly she gasped, "I see it! I see it!"

For a moment her husband stood in almost apoplectic silence, then as his temporary paralysis left, he hurried his wife out to their car and, without a word of farewell, beat a hasty retreat. I have often wondered if he ever took the time and effort to prove to himself whether his wife was right or wrong.

Another closed mind was evidenced upon the occasion of a dinner I attended. One of the other guests was a teacher whose reaction to the trend of our conversation was most uncomplimentary. He not only refused to join in the experiments, he was rude enough about it that he sat off to one side of the room reading a magazine while the rest of us were examining each others' "haloes." It happened that one of the other guests was a pupil of mine and about a week after the incident the pupil told me that he had seen the teacher several days after the dinner party. He said that the man was most caustic in his reference to our conversation of the evening in question. The young man said he asked the teacher if he had ever considered taking a look for himself. After much argument and protest, the skeptic finally agreed to take a few minutes to make a fair trial. Within three minutes he became a convert, prefacing his conversion with a flabbergasted "Well, I'll be darned, there are such things!"

ALL SUBSTANCES HAVE AN AURA

Since everything in the world of matter manifests in the form it does because it is a certain number of atoms or molecules held together by its own vibratory frequency, *everything, animate or inanimate, has an aura.* The human aura differs from others, including plant and animal auras, because of mental and spiritual differences. The only time I ever saw what appeared to be a human being without an aura was one of the strangest experiences of my life.

Briefly put, this man appeared from nowhere, gave information to a group of us concerning where and when to look for a spacecraft (which we saw exactly as he predicted), then left without explanation of who he was or why he had come with this message for us. Although he was quite ordinary in appearance, there was certainly something out of the ordinary about him—as soon as he stepped into the room I became so nauseated that I had to retreat quickly out into the night air. After about ten minutes I had sufficiently regained my composure to return to the group in the house. The mysterious visitor was seated on a couch directly across from the chair in which I had been sitting and after I resumed my place I was in an excellent position to observe him carefully. I first was aware of the fact that this man seemed to have difficulty looking directly at anyone to whom he spoke—his eyes just did not seem to be properly focused. Next I was startled to see that the auras of the two women on the couch with him were plainly visible, but there was none to be seen on him! A conference with our host confirmed the fact that there was no visible aura around the man. After the sighting which he had told us about, he dropped from sight for a while, although he did contact our host and tell him of two other flights—also sighted on schedule. Then he dropped out of contact with any of us for over a year. One more visit at that time with the host of the eventful evening was the last any of us heard of him. We knew no more about him after he was gone than we did when he first appeared.

The only explanation which has been forthcoming about this mysterious affair is that this man was probably from some other planet—his seeming inability to focus his eyes attributed to the fact that he was accustomed to looking in another dimension, and his apparent lack of an aura caused by the fact that his magnetic field was of a frequency far too high for us to see.

AURAS OF FLOWERS

Flowers have lovely auras; it is said that the violet has the most beautiful of all. As a flower fades, so does its color and fragrance. Color is vibration, and the fragrance is sent out on vibrational waves, which accounts for the diminishing of expanse of perfumed air around a fading flower.

ANIMAL AURAS

Animals have definite auras which reveal something of the temperament of the animal under study, and more than this is supposed to be revealed to advanced aura readers.

ESOTERIC IMPLICATION OF AURAS

Some of the higher esoteric schools maintain that a person who is highly evolved should not seal his aura, since this limits the ability to expand his consciousness out into the Cosmos. They feel that man is infinite in his consciousness and is finite when his aura encloses him in a sealed shell. Of course, anyone so highly evolved as to be infinite in his consciousness should not need too much protection from influences which would affect a more mundane soul.

Among American Indians the aura is recognized as a very real thing of inestimable value. Some tribes assert that every new-born baby is, in the first instant of life, marked with a cross of light showing on its forehead, indicative of its spiritual source and purity. This indication of freedom from sin, with the touch of God inherent in everyone from birth, makes the Indians cognizant of their responsibility and the privilege of parenthood.

The aura, too, is present from the moment of birth, and Indians recognize one particular area of the aura as clearly significant of family ties. According to those able to read the aura, it is an unfailingly accurate identification of the parents, and is more strongly like one of the parents than the other. Inadvertent "baby-switching" is thus unknown among Indians. (It has been claimed that in some states where the Indian population is high, Indians are sometimes called upon to settle possible mix-ups in some of our "civilized" hospitals.) The aura acquires predominantly personal expression at about the fifth year, as the personality and understanding of the child begins to alter the family influence.

Among many tribes marriage prospects are "aurically inspected" before permission to marry is granted. What a wonderful way to predetermine a couple's chance for happiness: if the aura colors are not indicative of harmony, the pair must try to make the necessary changes. If the dull red of sensuality is predominant this is considered a foreboding of impermanence.

Indians also recognize the aura as invaluable in the diagnosing of illness and the treatment needed. It is their belief that everyone is born with the ability to see auras, but only those who make a study of them are able to use the ability authoritatively.

The fact that auras appear on photographs gives one pause in considering the fear some primitive people exhibit when cameras are aimed in their direction. In some inexplicable manner they have concluded that a camera will capture a part of their spirit or life-force. (How have they determined this? When one tries to decide how this belief could have spread in societies where cameras are not a part of every household's equipment, it is hard to understand. Perhaps it is word of mouth reports from natives who have seen photographs and have seen the aura captured thereon.)

Auras *do* appear on photographs, and there are psychics who can do readings from photographs brought to them or mailed to them. It is asserted by the people who have this ability that the aura in the picture changes coincidentally with the subject's aura as long as the subject lives. A picture, for example, which was taken three years ago, does not show just what was in the aura at the time the shutter was snapped—it shows what the subject *is* at the time the reading is done. If the person in the photograph is no longer alive, no aura shows at all!

This interesting idea was tested in my home one evening when a woman, only slightly known to anyone present, allowed us to examine two photographs she had in her purse. The subjects in the pictures, both men, were apparently about the same age, both appeared to be vital and strong, yet one of the photographs had no aura while the other did. No one expressed reaction until each person present had had time to come to his own conclusion. Those experienced in seeing auras, without exception, concurred on which man had the aura and which did not. The photo with no visible aura was that of the woman's deceased husband, while that of the other man was a picture of the man to whom the woman was engaged. This was our first experiment of this nature, since the information was just presented to our attention that evening—and not by the woman who owned the pictures we examined. Here again, open-mindedness produced startling verification.

The complete study of the aura is one of the most interesting and beneficial that one can undertake. I hope that this chapter will open the door to many—may you enjoy testing the theories presented and derive full benefit from the protection of your own "shining armor of God," *your own aura!*

SUMMARY OF CHAPTER FOUR

1. The human aura is a personal force field, built, maintained and used by every individual; the more he understands it, the more benefit he may derive from it.
2. Anyone can see auras, including his own, by following the few simple rules set forth in this chapter.
3. There are some disadvantages to over-developed abilities to see auras.
4. Aura interpretation in its highest form is an involved and lengthy study.
5. With the observation of a few simple recommendations included in this chapter you can increase the effectiveness of your aura.
6. The aura can provide protection from physical, mental and emotional "attacks."
7. Aura contacting aura effects good or bad transfusions.
8. Auras show many colors, each of which has its own significance.

9. Auras always leave the body at death—sometimes in advance of death.

10. American Indians use auras effectively in matters of marriage suitability, proof of parenthood, and healing.

11. Auras appear on photographs and usually disappear at the time of death.

FIVE

Premonition and

Precognition

Through Psychism

Buried deep within the human consciousness there is an ability which occasionally enables man to project into the area where time and space do not exist. Common usage of the word "premonition" implies a glimpse into that area with the opportunity to see something disastrous or tragic moving from the future into the present. "Precognition," on the other hand, causes less concern since it, in its popular meaning, does not always give a preview of a coming calamity. It may even show the results of a Kentucky Derby or where you should go to meet your soul-mate.

As these experiences happen occasionally to almost everyone, it seems that we all have the necessary equipment; it's just a question of finding the right key for the switch, as developed in this chapter.

THE GIFT OF PROPHECY

Since the beginning of recorded time there have been seers and prophets who were so well developed along these lines that they were fluent and prolific in giving out accurate information and predictions. I doubt seriously that anyone can properly deny the reality of this gift—at least if he has given any thought at all to the recorded prophecies of either ancient times or current days. Although they aren't too common, there are enough accurate predictions on record to make it impossible to claim intelligently that precognition is not a genuine occurrence. It takes place often enough and with sufficient detail to render chance an unsatisfactory explanation.

Why predicted events may not have happened

There are two schools of thought on the reason for non-occurrence of predicted events. One concept is that to be forewarned is to be forearmed; thus one may avert a predicted disaster. The other concept is that predictions are not always accurate either because of misunderstanding of the message or incomplete reception of it. These, of course, are the explanations of those who accept the possibility of precognitive abilities—they do not satisfy non-believers.

In considering the fallibility of predictions, we are concerned with the battle over the extent of free will. How much of what happens to us is the result of our destiny, and how much of it is controlled by our own freedom of choice or decision? This is a controversy which has continued for centuries and will no doubt continue for many more.

If we have free will in everything, we are, of course, in complete control of the outcome of even those events which are presaged in precognitive experiences. If we do not like that of which we are apprised, we can change it by exercise of our will. If, on the other hand, we are creatures of predestiny, whose futures are fixed by a superior intelligence, the only excuse for an inaccurate prediction is the inability to use the gift of foreseeing efficiently.

I am inclined to take a middle-of-the-road view. I believe that precognition is a very real faculty, certainly undeveloped in most of us. Within certain limits we function under the free will concept. I also feel that there are some areas in our lives where we are subjected to certain experiences which are necessary to our opportunity to grow mentally, emotionally and spiritually. These are the types of experience we would avoid if we possibly could do so. In other words, it is my belief that we function under a law which gives us partial free will and partial fixed incidents which we must undergo. It is our reaction to predetermined events which is the measure of our spiritual and moral stature.

I do not believe that casual everyday experiences are in the category of the inevitable, unless they are a part of a necessary chain of events which will lead to a certain situation. Nor do I believe that our *reaction* to major portions of our life experiences is fixed in advance. For example, marriage might be a part of our destiny, perhaps even a bad marriage is inevitable in some instances; but it is up to us whether we overcome the difficulties and rise above them or allow the experience to destroy us.

THE FACTOR OF FREE WILL

The more we demonstrate our capability to react intelligently to situations and profit by our mistakes, the more free will enters into our lives. Increase of wisdom brings more latitude of choice. Just as a child in elementary school has little choice of subject matter to be studied, the same student, when he reaches college level, picks his own course of study and more or less pursues it as his own responsibility.

Since free will is a factor in some future activities, it is only reasonable that no one can infallibly predict the exact outcome of future events. There is a certain amount of predictability which presents itself, even to casual observers, because of existing personality traits or certain circumstances; that is, if a person laden with packages approaches a windy street corner, it is not unreasonable to predict that his hat will blow off as he makes the turn, particularly if the pedestrian involved is a man. However, it is a little less certain that the hat will fly off if the principal is a woman, because she may have taken the precaution to secure her hat in some unseen way.

Those prognostications which are based upon obvious circumstances or an understanding of personality are, of course, not genuine precognitive demonstrations. It is only when a prediction is made which contains information beyond the normal source of information relative to the event foreseen that the element of psychism enters.

Sometimes conditions pertinent to the health of a subject can be determined by a psychic. This may be attributed to a subconscious or superconscious recognition of existing health conditions which may or may not as yet be known to the subject being "read." Whereas such prevision would certainly be the result of so-called psychic ability, it still does not constitute true precognition, since the condition was discovered by a sensitivity which simply recognized it in its early stages before it became evident to the average normal awareness. If one predicts a health problem which will be the direct result of an accident which has not as yet occurred, this is precognitive.

PRECOGNITION VS. PSYCHIC IMPRESSION

In trying to distinguish between true precognition and a psychic impression which *appears* to be prophetic in nature, one finds that the dividing line is very thin. True precognition is correct divination, whereas psychism with regard to the future may or may not be accurate. It is the contention of spiritualists that impressions received with regard to future events originate in the world of spirit; some entity from the discarnate state communicates the information to a medium, who in turn passes it along. This in itself is an indication that the information received may or may not be accurate. The communicating spirit presumably could be in error, could deliberately mislead, or could be unable to pass the information along in such a manner as to make details perfectly clear.

Personally, I favor the theory that there is no such thing as time in space. Some events are recorded well in advance of the date of our awareness of them, and proper tuning to the right wave length makes these coming events known before they happen. I believe that the *inevitable* incidents, those in which free will does not play a part, or those which involve other than human control, are all portrayed vibrationally, well in advance of actual occurrence on our level of consciousness. I cannot offer any scientific (or even logical) explanation of my belief since I do not fully understand the Fourth Dimension, but the concept of spatial vibratory records of what we call the future impresses me the most.

A precognitive experience

A friend told me that her daughter had read, in that morning's local paper, a headline and story on the sports page which described a racing accident in which a friend of her husband had been killed the night before. My friend asked me if it was in my paper—she could not find it in hers.

There was no such story in my paper, so my friend called her daughter to ask for more details. When the daughter looked for the story she could not find it either.

During the course of that day the incident was discussed with a number of people.

The next morning the accident was reported in detail—but it had *happened* many hours after the young woman had read the story precognitively, although to her it was as if she had actually read it.

This is what must have been a true precognitive experience. This was not an event which could have been foreseen in any normal manner, nor could it have been just a "hunch," since the young woman had known the story in all its details.

Precognition via hypnotic trance

I have seen precognition demonstrated beyond question by persons in hypnotic trance. Each time the subjects, in very deep trance, were instructed to go ahead in time to a certain hour or day, well into the future from the time the experiments were conducted. The places and conditions under which the subjects were to find themselves were also stipulated.

The first subject, a woman, was told while in trance on Good Friday, that she was moving ahead to the following Sunday, which was Easter. She was told that she would be opening her morning newspaper and, when she scanned the front page, she would read one of the headlines aloud. At that time Cuba did not figure as prominently in the news as it has done in the past few years, so we were somewhat surprised when the five or six word headline she read concerned that country. At any rate, on the following Sunday morning there it was, exactly as she had given it!

The next experiment of this nature involved the same procedure, this time with another woman as a subject. We did not ask for a headline—just anything which caught her eye while looking over the front page. She was in deep trance but responded by repeating several times a name which meant nothing to anyone present at the time of the experiment. The subject herself said she had never heard of the name herself, when asked about it.

On the named day we carefully scanned the front page of the paper. We found no such name. We were just about to conclude that the experiment had been a failure when someone noticed the name in a small item at the bottom of the page. The item concerned a minor traffic violation, and the man against whom charges had been brought was the man whose name had been given. We could never understand why this particular item was of such interest to the subject since she did not know him.

I saw real precognition demonstrated by a person in trance during an experiment I conducted myself, with no third party present. A man who had been referred to me by a local hypnotist who knew of my interest in mind potentials was the subject. He was interested in obtaining some advance information. I do not ordinarily actively participate in this sort of experiment, but the man persuaded me that he was well versed in this sort of thing and merely wanted me to assist him in the proper conduct of his effort.

After a period of relaxation and guidance to the proper level of consciousness, I touched the man's forehead and asked for the information he was hopeful of obtaining. He answered clearly and without hesitation. Within two hours his response proved to be absolutely accurate.

This gentleman was interested in a form of speculation; I was interested in testing my theory about precognition; each of us obtained what we sought from the effort. I am satisfied that this is a most promising avenue to explore in the search for the key to the future.

Precognition via sleep state

Much of the precognitive or premonitional data recorded seems to come during the sleep state. It is usually connected with some sort of impending trouble, such as the death or serious illness of someone closely connected to the principal. These are frequently referred to as "precognitive dreams," since they most often present themselves during the sleep state, either as sleep is approaching, during deep sleep or during the semi-conscious state of the awakening process. As a general thing they are of a premonitional or warning nature, but there are reports of impressions which are not so disastrous in essence.

In order to clarify my statement that I believe that there is no such thing as time in space, yet state that I have seen consciousness projected ahead to specifically named dates, I should like to say here that I do not think that time exists as we know it. I feel that translation takes place—it is as if an interpreter clarifies what is expected or expressed. When we are in the sleep state and have a precognitive or premonitional dream, something in our conscious-ness makes the time known in terms we can understand with our conscious mind.

Establishing validity of precognitive experience

In order to prove the validity of a precognitive experience, whether it be in form of a dream or a "vision" during the waking state, there are some requirements set up by most research groups. One of the first rules is that the information must be written down in detail as soon as possible after it has been received. Then the report must be signed by several reliable witnesses, or it must immediately be recorded on a postcard or any other type of corre-spondence material which results in the postmark cancellation ap-pearing on the main body of the message, then mailed without delay. The report should be mailed either to a research group interested in the value of such information or it may be self-addressed. The important point is the postmark or witnessed and dated evidence that the information was precognitively received. Do not enclose the information about the experience on a separate sheet of paper enclosed in an envelope—*this does not constitute proof.*

Anyone who frequently has precognitive experiences should make a habit of so recording his prophetic disclosures. They are of value to the interest of research only if they are in evidential form.

A prophetic dream

Recently I met a woman who had a high degree of sensitivity which unfortunately was neither understood nor appreciated, nor was it cultivated or refined sufficiently to be more beneficial than detrimental.

She told me of a prophetic dream she had had a few years earlier. This was not properly recorded at the time, so it has no value in research, but it is an interesting example of a truly precognitive dream.

In her dream, this woman saw an elderly widower of her acquaintance in his new place of business in another town. The gentleman was a jeweler. She noticed a number of unusual pieces of jewelry in his showcase. She heard him say that he had married a woman she did not know, but she clearly heard the name of the new wife. This old gentleman's home and business were in a town about 1,400 miles away from the home of the principal, who had never seen them.

Many months after she had the dream, the woman was in the town she had dreamed of previously. She went into the jewelry shop to call on her old friend. There her entire dream was acted out in full detail: she saw the same pieces of jewelry and the announcement was given of the man's marriage to the woman named in her dream.

I am positive that this was a true report, but unfortunately it cannot be used as an evidential case since it, as so many other similar cases, was not properly verified and documented.

There is no doubt that multitudes of people have had equally genuine precognitive dreams, but they too are lost to research for the same reason. The time and effort to record them and the few cents a postcard costs are negligible compared to the value of such proof. Sheer numbers of such accountings would prove beyond question that precognition is a fruitful area of investigation.

It is up to the layman to give scientists the proper evidence in sufficient quantity to promote the growing interest and to continue to offer incentive. If any of us have a dream which we have any reason to feel might have some possibility of becoming a reality, we should record it properly. This is equally true of any impression or vision we might have.

Role of the subconscious mind

Since most precognitive impressions seem to come when the principal is either in a sleep state or in a state of detachment—in other words, the precognitive impression is not usually received through a conscious effort—it would appear that the subconscious mind or the superconscious mind must be activated in order to see into the area of future events. I believe that properly used hypnotic techniques, employed with promising subjects, will do much to reveal the proper method to develop the faculty.

"Second sight"

In some parts of the world precognition is referred to as "second sight." This is particularly true in Scotland, where this ability is somewhat common, and has the peculiar feature of being inherited. Even in this century, there is scarcely a family in Scotland which cannot claim at least one seer in its ranks—usually the seventh son of a seventh son, a formula which is considered infallible.

There is also the precognitive ability of countless natives in a certain area of Norway. This particular form of precognition manifests as an awareness of the arrival of a family member considerably in advance of the actual physical arrival. All sounds, such as wheels on a driveway, keys turning in locks, doors opening and closing, footsteps, etc., are clearly heard many minutes, and in some cases hours, before the person physically appears on the scene. This is such a common and unfailing sign that many women use this as a timing indicator for the preparation and serving of meals.

I talked with one man from this part of Norway. He told me that his mother always knew 25 minutes before his father would come in from work. This seemed to be the time it would take his father to travel the distance between his place of business and his home. He said that every member of his family could hear the wheels on the drive and the key in the lock as clearly during the illusory arrival as during the actual.

Can it be that there is something significant about the topography of this certain part of the world? Is it simply because it has taken place here so frequently that the natives *believe* in it so strongly that it continues to happen? It sometimes happens in a limited area of Scotland, but not with the startling frequency with which it occurs in Norway.

Precognition can be demonstrated in telekinesis

Precognitive ability is often demonstrated to a remarkable degree in telekinesis tests which involve cards, dice or pictures; in fact, the preguessing is frequent enough that a name has been chosen to designate the occurrence—displacement. A few principals in such tests have demonstrated an amazing faculty for naming the card, number or picture to be turned before the one responsible for the turns or throws has even laid a hand on the object involved in the test. This particular manifestation of foreknowledge is discussed in Chapter Six.

An unusual case of precognition

One day I was sitting at my desk in my shop doing automatic writing while reading a book. As mentioned in the section of this book which has to do with automatism, it was not unusual for the writing to foretell the arrival of a customer or a friend. As was my custom, I did not read what had been written until the writing process stopped. On this particular occasion when the writing ceased and I picked up the paper to read what had been written, I found that it said that I was to have a strange new customer in a few minutes.

Almost as soon as I had finished reading the message, a woman walked in the door. I knew at first glance that this was indeed a new customer—and the word "strange" had been fittingly used also!

Since this took place some time ago, some of the reasons her appearance could be called "strange" would no longer attract attention, but at the time she could have turned anyone's head for a second look.

She was under five feet tall, dressed completely in black, and attractive in a curiously repelling way. Her costume was a modified Chinese jacket and pants, black slippers and jet jewelry. Her hair, equally black, was done in Chinese style with ornaments projecting from a large "bun." Her eye make-up was black, with heavily accented and almost wing-like eyebrows—not too startling in view of the current fads of strange eye paint, but I believe this would attract some attention even today.

She began to tell me of her interest in the occult and her participation in a devil-worshipping cult in Paris. She was most interesting and told me of some of her adventures and accomplishments, including some experiences in her course of study in Tibet and other centers of mysticism throughout the world.

A peculiar thing happened to her, she said, ever since her involvement with the French group; each time she told or heard a truth (or as she put it, "stood in the presence of truth"), she would get goose flesh all over. During our conversation she would occasionally hold out her arm and show the bumps which kept coming and going during our conversation.

She told me an interesting precognitive experience she had had recently. I do not recall the time of the event but it could not have been too far back in her life as she was still in her early twenties.

Her parents were divorced, and at the time of this episode she was living in New York with her father. She had an aunt, a sister of her mother, of whom she was very fond. One day she had a strong feeling that her aunt was in some sort of trouble, and she seemed to see her with her unusually beautiful face horribly distorted.

She said she had no idea where her aunt was, but for some reason she told her father that she wanted to fly to Miami, Florida, without delay. She caught a plane, and it was not until she stepped into a taxi at the Miami airport that she had any idea of what she should do next. Then, she said, she heard herself tell the taxi driver that she wanted to go to one of Miami's large hospitals.

As she entered the hospital she seemed to know just where to go. In one of the upper corridors, where she found herself without any inquiry at the reception desk, she saw a nun and asked if her aunt was in a certain room. She was told that her aunt was indeed in that room, having been brought in after suffering a stroke while walking on one of the main shopping streets.

When she went into the room she found her aunt lying there with her face frozen in a dreadful grimace, exactly as she had appeared to the girl in her vision in New York!

The timing was such that she was alerted to this tragic event immediately before it happened. She explained to me that this was not the first time that she had foreknowledge of impending situations, nor was it the only time she had experienced the unseen guidance which took her to the proper place at the proper time.

To add further interest to her story, she was a young woman from a family whose name is internationally known, so verification would not have been difficult had I had any reason to disbelieve her story.

There is no area more tantalizing and more resistant to understanding in the field of psychical research than that which involves the investigation of precognition. It is extremely difficult to produce the phenomenon under controlled conditions; there is not sufficient evidence available to show what conditions might be conducive to producing it, even to a limited degree.

Dr. Gardner Murphy, Director of Research at the Meninger

Clinic in Topeka, Kansas, in a lecture before the Conference of the Parapsychology Forum in New York in December of 1959, suggested that perhaps the hypnotic technique held much promise as a means of inducing such experiences. He, as do all responsible researchers, feels that only thoroughly trained hypnotists and qualified interrogators should conduct such tests.

As previously stated I feel that hypnosis does hold the key to help bring us light on the future. I also feel that it is not advisable to use this tool lightly—it is not a parlor game, it could be dangerous, and it is of no value, anyway, if the results are not properly recorded and evaluated.

SUMMARY OF CHAPTER FIVE

1. Man can project into the timeless-spaceless dimension.
2. Free will or predestination—either may alter the accuracy of predictions.
3. Precognition can be spontaneous or induced.
4. To be accepted as evidence of valid precognition, experiences must be properly recorded or documented.
5. Incidence of precognition is high in Scotland and Norway.
6. Generally speaking, premonition is a term used for the more emotionally involved experience which forebodes disaster or tragedy in the future.

SIX

Psychokinesis and

Telekinesis – Power of

Mind over Matter

"Psychokinesis" and "telekinesis" are two words used to designate the phenomena which involve the movement of material objects with no visible or physical source of power, with their control through the result of conscious mental force alone. These terms may be applied to such manifestations as table-tilting, rappings, levitation, dice control, some poltergeist activity, and on and on through a long list of phenomena of a sort which affect solid or material objects, the principles of which will be discussed in this chapter.

Since poltergeist activity and dice throwing tests conducted by parapsychologists are the most widely publicized and most familiar to the greatest number of people, these two aspects will be dealt with first.

THE ENIGMA OF THE POLTERGEIST

The word "poltergeist," derived from the German "Polter Geist" which means rattling ghost, is defined in one dictionary as a "ghost or spirit that makes its presence known by any kind of clatter, as knocking and the noises of moving objects." The approach now used in the observation and evaluation of poltergeist incidents is usually one which excludes the phantom theory. Instead it attributes the phenomena to a human element, either spontaneous or deliberate, a result of some kind of mental activity.

Spiritualistic interpretation of the poltergeist phenomena asserts that the objects are moved by a mysterious force which emanates from the body of a sensitive, this force controlled or manipulated by intelligences independent of the medium. There are some proponents of the latter theory who claim that the exhibition of control of mind over matter can, upon occasion, be deliberately produced and controlled by certain mediums. This would seem to indicate that there are times when a medium, through use of this force, is the director of, rather than the channel for, the attending spirits.

In any event, poltergeist activity occurs frequently, as is evidenced by numerous accounts in news media and periodicals which specialize in reports of psychical exploration, experiences and research, such as Chimes, Fate, Tomorrow, etc.

Although I do not consider my house haunted, I will share an experience with you of a phenomenon which I must classify as poltergeist activity. I do not know the source of the manifestation—all I am certain of is that it actually happened. Certain objects flew through the air with no visible aid to propel them, and there was much noise for the duration of the activity. Hence, this was a poltergeist at work.

A poltergeist activity

One Sunday, my daughter was brought to my home from the hospital after the birth of her first child. From the time she and the baby arrived until 11:45 P.M., the house was filled with visiting friends and relatives. Since the new mother was experiencing some difficulty as a result of anaesthesia and found it hard to get in and out of the soft bed in the bedroom, I had made up a bed for her on a sofa in the living room. This improvised bed backed up to a built-in set of shelves containing about 60 books and assorted bric-a-brac. The baby's bassinet was placed alongside the sofa near the head of it. My own bedroom is across a little hall from the living room. Lights left on in two rooms illuminated the living room sufficiently for us to see clearly in the event we had to move around in the night to attend the baby.

Both my daughter and I were in a state of almost total exhaustion, and she had gone deeply to sleep before I even went into my bedroom. I had decided not to undress immediately because I feared that if I were too comfortable, I would sleep too soundly to hear if my daughter called in the night.

I stretched out on my bed and was just about to fall asleep when I heard a resounding thud from the living room. It is no exaggeration to say that I leaped out of bed and ran into the living room. In the subdued light I could plainly see my daughter still in deep sleep, her position unchanged from the time I had left her a few minutes before. The baby was sleeping in his bassinet alongside. *But* right in the middle of the floor, about eight feet away from the shelves was an open book!

The relative position of my daughter to the books made it impossible for her to have reached them without getting out of bed and, of course, a five day old baby was hardly a logical suspect.

Too tired to even wonder how it got into the middle of the floor, I picked the book up, put it back into place without even looking at it, and staggered off to bed again.

I had no sooner gotten back on my bed when I heard two more thuds! Once again I dashed back out into the living room to see what had happened this time, and there lay *two* books in the same place the first one had landed. As I was putting the second of these back onto the shelf, it suddenly penetrated my tired brain that this was no doubt a poltergeist at work.

I looked at the title of the book still in my hand; it was the heavy volume, *The Complete Works of O. Henry*. With the exception of two dictionaries, this was the heaviest book on the shelves.

In retrospect I was furious with myself for not noting the places where the books were open and for not looking at the titles of each. Could they have been trying to tell me something? All three of the books had been open when I picked them up and I am sure that if I had not been so foggy with fatigue I would have been more alert to the phenomenal nature of the whole affair. I do wish I hadn't missed the boat the only time I ever had personal contact with a poltergeist. For the rest of the night I slept in the living room, but there was no further activity.

I know that my daughter had not moved, for when it finally dawned on me that the incident was out of the ordinary I looked carefully at her long hair as it was spread on the pillow and it was just as it had been when I had left the room about ten minutes previously. It would have been impossible for her to settle into a horizontal position, let alone arrange her hair and the covers, in the time it took me to fly out at the sound of the impacts.

I do not know why it happened on that particular evening; I just know that it happened exactly as I have described it. Except for being extraordinarily tired, I was in a state of completely normal consciousness.

REPORTS OF POLTERGEISTS DATE BACK TO 856 B.C.

It seems to be characteristic of poltergeists to display childish prankishness, although there have been cases recorded where the manifestations took on a malicious and even dangerous or threatening nature. Reports of activities of this sort are abundant, dating as far back at 586 B.C., according to the research of a man named Lang, author of *Cock Lane and Common Sense*.

The Wesley family, of Epworth, England, left what may be considered the most complete account of extensive poltergeist activities ever recorded. For the benefit of anyone who wishes to read about this famous case of the haunting of the parsonage in which this well-known religionist family lived, most of the accounts of it are classified in reference books under the heading of either Epworth or Wesley.

I do not recall having read of much personal injury sustained during poltergeist incidents, but certainly there is much evidence of real destructiveness. In innumerable instances objects have been hurled with such force as to cause them to be shattered or damaged to an extent which made repair impossible or impractical. In other cases objects have been merely displaced or moved from one spot to another with enough control to result in no impairment or damage. At times witnesses have stated that the objects floated gently from one spot to another, defying the law of gravity, but most frequently the objects move with such force as to give the impression that they have been hurled with some force comparable to physical strength.

CLOSE RELATION OF POLTERGEIST AND DICE-THROWING TESTS

At first thought it seems that there is a considerable gap between poltergeist activity and the dice-throwing tests in the investigation of psychokinesis. Unless one accepts the spiritualistic theory of the former phenomenon, there is a very close relationship between the two, in that the control of the force which appears to stop the dice rolls at the proper time could be the same kind of control which activates the movement of objects in poltergeist manifestations. If there is in the human mind a force which can control or dictate which faces of the dice will be upturned, it is not unreasonable to assume that the same force can dictate the placement and displacement of other objects.

The records of psychical researchers are liberally laced with accounts of the observations of movements of objects, such as tables and other articles of furniture, in the presence of mediums who had no apparent physical contact with the pieces so moved. Test conditions proved that some of the manifestations were fraudulent, but there was a sufficient number that were inexplicable to lend credence to the psychokinetic theory.

In dice tests the dice are usually tumbled in a wire cage or a dice cup, and ejected onto a table padded so the dice will tumble, roll or bounce freely and placed so there is a backdrop or wall in order to prevent the dice from falling to the floor.

Instead of a table, one may use a shallow box which has been padded and is securely in place so that it does not shift around during the experiments.

The dice used must be as well balanced as possible, and for this reason most investigators prefer the kind of dice which have inlaid spots as opposed to those which are merely painted.

A SIMPLE DICE CONTROL TEST

A simple test is one in which the subject tries to get one number to turn up as many times as he possibly can in a series of 12 runs. For example, let us suppose that the test is conducted with a single pair of dice. The subject has selected one number which he will attempt to turn face up as often as possible, perhaps the number 5; so as the dice are shaken and thrown he concentrates on the number 5. He *wills* it to turn up and *believes* success will follow.

It is well to try the tests in two ways—both with the subject himself making the throws and with a second party handling the dice at all times.

Each throw of the dice is tabulated, record being made of each number that shows on the faces of the dice. For each face showing the target number, he gets credit for a hit and if both are the chosen number in a single throw he gets credit for two hits. At the end of 12 throws, the total of correct hits indicates his percentage of success on the basis that four hits out of 12 throws is chance; anything over four hits in the run of 12 is evidence of possible mental control.

Of course, one set of runs does not prove anything conclusive unless the result is phenomenally high, so for this reason it is best to go through at least three runs of 12 throws each.

There are variations to this test, such as using as a target number one which can only be the result of the total of two faces, such as a 7 total showing on each roll. In this test, anything over two correct throws in the series of 12 is above chance. In throwing pairs, such as two of any specified number in each throw, in a series of 36 runs, if the subject gets more than one pair of the number designated this is above chance.

ADVANCED TESTS TO CONTROL DICE NUMBERS

If one desires to work more seriously in this line of investigation, six dice may be used at once instead of two. The number of dice used does not seem to change the ability to control them, but it does shorten by a considerable amount the time involved in getting sufficient runs to provide conclusive evidence. In the use of six dice, chance is then based upon one hit in every throw if a single face is called, or one chance in six, just as it is in the single pair tests. The single number throws are always based on the fact that one-sixth equals chance.

In the testing laboratories such as Professor Rhine's, as many as 48 dice may be used in each throw, but this is much too involved and requires equipment beyond that which is found in the average household. Since this is a handbook for laymen, I suggest that the most practical tests for the average reader are the ones using not more than three pairs of dice at a time. The results are just as telling since the scoring is on a percentage basis, but the huge numbers for statistics demanded by science are lacking.

Remember that in conducting the tests, the subject concentrates very hard and through sheer will attempts to cause the correct faces to turn, always keeping in mind the same number for at least 24 possible hits.

Basic rules

Here are a few rules for the conduct of tests:

1. The dice should never be held in the hand for the throws; a cup for holding and shaking them should be used.

2. The same dice should be used throughout the entire run of any target number; never change dice once the run starts.

3. If a die or some dice fall on the floor by some chance, these are not counted. The whole throw is disregarded and a new throw must be made. This is also a general rule if a die or some dice stop in a cocked position against the edge of the backdrop or each other.

4. The target number must be specified in advance of the first throw of the run.

5. To insure that the control is exerted by the subject being tested rather than by anyone else who might be present it is a good idea to have the subject be the only one aware of the target number in some of the tests. This may be done by having him draw a number or by having him record the number where no one else can see it after he has silently chosen one mentally.

This control by will alone is a difficult thing to accomplish, but it is an interesting and entertaining pastime quite often used in social gatherings purely for its entertainment value.

If used seriously and for investigative purposes, remember that fatigue and boredom take their toll and cut down on the rate of control, so don't overdo the tests at any time. A few complete series of three or four target numbers will suffice for one person as a beginning, and if the interest seems to be sustained without a loss in hits scored, they may be continued. But be on the alert for signs of lessening interest and call a halt before discouragement sets in.

TABLE TILTING

Another means of practicing to develop telekinesis (although there will no doubt be disagreement from both spiritualists and even the opposing factions about this one) is table tilting. This involves the attempt to levitate a table or other article of furniture by simply placing the hands lightly on the surface and willing it to move. Although there is actual physical contact made, the movement which can result does not appear to be caused by any physical effort made on the part of the experimenters.

I have never had the experience of "sitting" at a table that levitated completely off the floor, but I have upon numerous occasions been with a table that walked all over a room, and on two different times was at a table that walked from one room to another and back again. This really makes an exciting experience—imagine a group of people solemnly following a table from room to room, each person going through the necessary bodily contortions to maintain hand contact with the surface of a galloping table! Sometimes the pace is undulating and slow; at other times it is a rapid movement.

As is my custom when participating in any of the tests of potential extrasensory ability, I do not work with anyone whose motives I suspect or who has an inclination to practical jokes. To me it would be an utter waste of time to participate in the fraud of any of these tests; I have nothing to gain by helping anyone to consciously (or unconsciously) perpetrate fraud. My only motive is my own curiosity about the natural laws which make these manifestations possible, to see how much of it is available to Mr. and Mrs. Average American, and how to make it more useful.

Serious aspects of table tilting

Although table tilting is frowned on by many people as either elementary or dangerous, I know many intelligent and cultured people who participate in it, either as a test of telekinetic strength or as a means of communication—with discarnate entities, according to some, and with the deeper consciousness, according to others. I have a great respect for anyone with the courage of his convictions and, regardless of his purpose in sitting, if he is serious and tasteful in his approach I admire him. I will sit with anyone who is conscientiously attempting to prove either survival, the ability to communicate with discarnates, or the power of mind over matter.

A lively session of table tilting

The most lively activity I ever saw during a table tilting session was as follows. Two friends and I had gone to Tampa, Florida, on a quest for some demonstrations by recommended mediums, one of whom was said to have extraordinary strength as a physical medium. She was very gracious but did not impress us too much, although I must admit that *some* of the things we saw during the session conducted in broad daylight seemed to be genuine enough. When we asked her about table tilting, she readily agreed to sit with us.

The table she used for this demonstration was an ordinary card table, the type with folding legs. She had each of us place our hands on the table top, with the fingers spread out and with as little pressure as possible. We were all standing, one at each side of the table. The medium began addressing someone she told us was her "spirit guide."

Almost immediately the table began to undulate, soon moved back and forth in a rocking motion, then changed directions at her spoken command. At her order the table literally galloped all over the room, changing pace each time she suggested that it do so. The action was lively and so responsive to her directions that we suspected some sort of chicanery, but we could see nothing to support our suspicions. Now that I am more versed in telekinetic phenomena, I can accept that this is no doubt what took place. In fact, since that time I have participated in similar experiments with such remarkable results that I know these things do happen.

TABLE TILTING CODES

Those who sit at a table with the purpose of communicating with discarnates have a code by which they determine the meaning of the messages they receive. There are some variations among individuals, but generally the pattern is as follows:

As the table rocks back and forth the feet of the table legs strike the floor, sometimes with resounding thumps, but always with enough force to be readily heard. "Yes," "no," and "maybe" are usually three, two and one thumps, in that order; in other words, "yes" is three thumps, "no" is two and "maybe" is one. For questions which cannot be answered so simply or for messages which may be spontaneously forthcoming, a different procedure is followed.

The code then may be that the letters of the alphabet are called out slowly and the thump will come on the intended letter, or more commonly, perhaps, the table will rock with each letter called out and will stop abruptly at the right call. Regardless of the method used or the source of the force which causes this activity, I have witnessed and participated in many interesting message sittings, during which intelligible "communications" were received.

I do not claim to know the exact nature of the power which causes and controls the action. I have read and heard many "experts" expounding high sounding explanations, but I do not recall of one who had a provable theory. To deny that it can happen is to take the easy way out. One who has sat and witnessed evidential information being received cannot help but wonder whether the sitters are experiencing in-depth probing of their own consciousness or actual contact with other entities. However, table tilting is a fact—and you also can help produce it!

TABLE TILTING TECHNIQUES

Success is most probable when the same people sit at the same table repeatedly over a reasonable length of time. The initial attempts should not exceed 20 minutes to a half hour at one time. These sittings should not take place more than once or twice a week. Sometimes the table responds noticeably during the first attempt— but this is not too common.

In an advanced research group I attended, we were told of two sisters who owned a nest of three tables, only one of which would respond at all to their tilting efforts. Both of these sisters were extremely psychic and well versed in many phases of mediumship. They brought the cooperative table to one of the sessions of the research group (which was sponsored by the Broward County Adult Education Program). The small wooden table responded readily and in a lively manner, regardless of the sitters, who took turns. Why would this table alone, of the three, respond?

I was told a number of years ago by a woman of my acquaintance that her husband and two of his friends during his boyhood decided to experiment with table tilting or levitation. They were doing this in the home of one of the other boys, without the knowledge of anyone else, as the home was unoccupied during the afternoon hours.

They had excellent results and were engrossed in their project one afternoon when the older brother of the boy at whose home they met came in unexpectedly. The young man who surprised them was outspoken in his ridicule of them and was tormenting them with rude and sarcastic remarks when, suddenly, he began to struggle and call for help in a panic-stricken voice.

The younger boys thought he was still tormenting them since they could see no reason for his scuffling about nor his terror. Then it appeared that he was about to be thrown bodily out of a window in the room. They went to his assistance and rescued the young fellow from some force which apparently had seized him in reprisal for his skeptical attitude. This experience with a ghostly "bouncer" brought all such experiments to an end for this particular group of boys.

UNEXPLAINED DISAPPEARANCE OF OBJECTS

There is one type of phenomenon which I will include here, although it may not rightly belong in this category of mind over matter. It seems to me to be so closely allied to poltergeist activity or possibly a result of telekinesis that I feel this is the best place to introduce it. It is the unexplained disappearance of objects.

Some time ago I read about a woman who was starting to compile a record of the many stories she had heard about objects which mysteriously disappeared, seemingly evaporating or dematerializing. So far as I know she has not as yet done this—but I wish she would because it would be fascinating reading for occult guidance.

This is something which happens to all of us at some time or other, but it seems so impossible that we are prone to dismiss the disappearance as plain loss, misplacement or poor memory. It is not until the circumstances are so remarkably strange as to command attention that we are apt to accept the idea that here is something more than meets the eye.

A totally incomprehensible thing of this sort happened to me in my own home. There were three of us in the room at the time—my mother-in-law, my daughter and I. My mother-in-law was sitting in a chair about ten feet away from me, and my daughter was about 14 feet away in another chair. Both chairs were on the opposite side of the room from the sofa on which I was sitting with my knitting. The telephone was at my right on a table at the far end of the sofa. We were all watching TV.

As I neared the end of one of the rows of my knitting the telephone rang. I quickly finished the few remaining stitches, put my knitting down, stepped to the end of the couch and picked up the phone. I stood with my back to the knitting while I spoke to the caller. My mother-in-law and my daughter never moved from their chairs, which were to my left as I stood talking on the phone.

When the telephone conversation was over I turned to take up my knitting again. I couldn't believe my eyes! The free needle, of brilliant aluminum (cerise in color), was gone! I had laid it across the piece of knitting when I put the work down. No one in the room had moved and yet that needle had vanished.

We did all of the obvious things; we looked behind, under and in the sofa, which was the Early American type with loose cushions on a maple frame. We searched the whole room. No needle!

The next day we searched even more thoroughly, even looking under the rug. That needle was gone! After hours of fruitless search, I finally went out and bought another pair of needles so I could finish my work. I still live in the same house and that needle has never been found. As far as I am concerned it simply dematerialized. How or why I do not know—but I am very grateful for the two witnesses to the fact that it *did* happen.

A local businessman told me that he quite frequently goes through the trying and mysterious disappearance and reappearance of his tools. He attributes the activity to poltergeists, although there is never any tossing about of the articles. They just disappear from his bench as he works and are returned when he says firmly, "All right now—you put that back!" He has a one man shop and, although this sounds unbelievable, he swears that it happens. I would be the last one in the world to dispute the possibility, although I have never witnessed such cooperative poltergeists.

This sort of thing seems to be closely allied to the phenomenon of apports. Spiritualists explain an apport as a gift from a spirit. It is, they explain, an object which has been irretrievably lost by someone, found by a spirit, dematerialized for transporting, then re-materialized in the presence of the person to whom he wishes to present it as a gift or a means of identification.

Although fraud has been proven many times during test seances held by researchers, here again we have the type of phenomenon which *has* been produced under the most stringent test conditions. It has happened frequently enough under the closest scrutiny that some researchers accept apportation as a reality.

SEANCES TO PRODUCE APPORTS

During some seances conducted for the purpose of producing apports, some of the objects received by sitters are of sufficient monetary value as to make it impractical for a medium to acquire them, only to pass them out to a sitter who has paid very little to sit in on the seance.

I have seen lovely pieces of jewelry which were received during apport seances, including a very old and beautiful amethyst received by an aunt of mine. The fee for the sitting was three dollars; the stone she received was worth several hundreds. This stone, which she received purportedly as a gift from my deceased uncle, brought much comment and questioning from the jeweler to whom she took it to have it mounted in a ring. He said it was a most unusual cut, one which had not been done for many years, and was of rare quality. He also asked her where she had ever found such a stone. She simply said that her husband had given it to her. I wonder what he would have said had she told him how she really did get it!

Sitting in on an apport seance can be a most interesting experience. The nature of the apports ranges from fresh flowers to live birds and fish, jewels, items that have a special significance to the sitter who receives them, and just plain *junk*. Beware of the apport medium who continuously gives out just worthless baubles and only occasionally produces items of some value. It surely cannot take any more effort on the part of a spirit with the capability of producing an apport to find one of value or significance than it would to bring a piece of junk which has no meaning, value or beauty. I'd feel highly indignant if any of the spirits I knew felt that I'd be impressed by a piece of junk as a token of their love and esteem, unless the piece has some symbolic meaning to them and to me.

One example of a worthless but meaningful apport was given to the wife of one of my cousins during a seance. It was a piece of whetstone, supposedly brought to her by an uncle who had been an inveterate whittler. This was most evidential so far as she was concerned since she was the only person in the room to whom a whetstone had any particular significance. She was sure that the medium knew nothing about her uncle, and the medium would hardly introduce such an object to impress a woman.

After one attends an apport seance it is easy to see why it is necessary to check the reputation of the medium in charge thoroughly before one accepts anything that occurs at face value.

THE TELEPORTING PHENOMENA

Very much like apporting is teleporting. This is the ability, occasionally demonstrated by mentalists, to cause material objects to dematerialize in one place and rematerialize in another. The primary difference between teleports and apports is that one is supposedly transferred from a known spot to another known spot by a living person using mental power, while the other is brought from an unknown spot to a known spot by a discarnate entity using less understood means.

It is claimed that there are, and have been for many years, holy men who have had the ability of teleporting themselves. This is aside from astral projection and bi-location. It is the ability to change the rate of vibration of the atoms of the body to such a high frequency that the body loses its density so that it can pass through matter, instantly be transported to a desired location, and then reduce the rate of vibration to the point where the body again becomes of normal density.

While it may sound fantastic, there are many reports of observing teleportation in psychic journals.

Teleporting experiences

Some years ago a young man who was active in some of the group work in which I was involved at that time had an experience which seemed to be spontaneous teleportation of his body. No one acquainted with him doubted the account as he gave it; he was genuinely mystified and shocked by it.

He, his wife, and two children were in their home watching television late one evening. His little son wanted a pillow, so the young father went into the bedroom to get one for him. About 90 seconds later he was at the front door, calling to be let in from the *outside*.

The floor plan of the house is such that it would have been impossible for him to have gone outside in any normal fashion without his family seeing him, since the bedroom wing of the house had no exits. The only doors to the outside had to be reached by going through the living room. The witnesses swore that he did not come back into the room after he went into the bedroom wing, until he was let in through the front door into the living room. All of the windows in the house were the jalousie type, impossible to crawl through without removal of slats and screen.

He said he had no idea what happened. He bent over to pick up a pillow from the bed and the next thing he knew he was outside in the yard, in a daze, with the pillow clutched in his arms.

I talked with him about 24 hours after it happened. He was still shaken by the incident and said that he had tried to remember everything about his trend of thought and action at the time this extraordinary thing took place. He could come up with nothing unusual except that it had happened.

EXTRAORDINARY USES OF TELEPORTATION

For some time now, we have been hearing and reading intimations and obscure references to the use of mental powers in the extrasensory manner in espionage work. Teleportation and bi-location are included in this, along with astral projection. Some of the reports have come from what might be termed unimpeachable sources—and I, for one, can believe it. I not only believe that it can be done, I think it is a most practical practice—if it can be understood and made to work when necessary. The ramifications of such application of what must be a natural law (or it would *never* work) are unlimited, and I can well imagine that it would be much more comfortable to be in an enemy territory under these circumstances than any other.

SUMMARY OF CHAPTER SIX

1. "Mind over matter" applications occur from poltergeist activities to dice throwing.
2. Objects often fly across a room with no apparent means of propulsion.
3. Dice tests and table tilting are simple means of experimenting with telekinesis.
4. In all tests with telekinesis you should be certain of the motivation and sincerity of your fellow experimenters.
5. Disappearing objects may be related to the telekinetic force.
6. Apports and teleportation, with or without mediums present, appear to be the result of application of the law of mind over matter.
7. Espionage work utilizes telekinesis with increasing frequency.

Automatism:

What It Means

in Psychism

A dictionary gives five meanings to the word "automatism," four of which are relative to the meaning referred to in this chapter.

1. The state or quality of being automatic or of having no voluntary action; specifically, the philosophical theory of the self-motion of phenomena.

2. Involuntary movements, whether or not accompanied by consciousness, which are centrally initiated, as distinguished from those which are reflex; also, the state or condition accompanying such subconscious phenomena.

3. Suspension of the conscious mind, especially reason and esthetic and moral preoccupation in order to release for expression the repressed ideas and images of the subconscious.

4. The capacity of independently originating action or motion.

Spiritualists attribute the controlling force in automatic phenomena to disembodied spirits; most researchers in the scientific investigation of physical manifestations of this sort attribute the control to the subconscious or superconscious mind of the automatist himself.

HOW AUTOMATISM MANIFESTS ITSELF

Generally speaking, automatism in this field manifests in the form of writing, drawing, painting, or in the demonstration of a dexterity, strength or knowledge *beyond the normal capacity of the individual to perform such feats.* Some automatists can only produce this phase of psychism while under trance or semi-trance, while others perform in a state of consciousness which appears to be perfectly normal. In either case there appears to be no awareness of what is to be done next during the production of automatic phenomena.

Strictly speaking, the Ouija Board may be termed an instrument of automatism, but since it is discussed at great length in a separate chapter, it will not be included for discussion at this time.

Automatic and inspirational writing

Many times, in the discussion of automatic manifestation, I have had it called to my attention that there is much confusion in some minds about the difference between automatic writing and inspirational writing.

When one is working automatically in writing, composing, painting, or whatever, there is no consciousness of what is to come next; for example, if one is painting automatically there is no knowledge of where the next stroke will be placed nor which color will be used. In automatic writing, one does not know what the next word will be or, in some cases, even the next letter; frequently, unless he reads as he writes, he will not know what has been written until the writing has ended. The automatist will be, very likely, in a perfectly normal state of consciousness—completely aware of conversation or activity around him.

There have been cases where the writer has put down words in a language unknown to him, has written out evidential information about matters completely beyond his knowledge, or pertinently given a description of persons or places completely strange to him.

Inspirational work, on the other hand, is done with complete awareness of what is to be done next. The idea comes for a melody, painting or literary work. It is heard or seen in its complete likeness, as a rule, and then the principal translates it into physical form. Inspirational work has contributed much to the beauty of our world, as most people realize. What is not understood is that automatism has done its share also.

In the field of literature, there are many well-known authors who are believed to have received much, if not all, of their works automatically. Two of the best known are Victor Hugo and Goethe.

Others include Sardou, Stainton Moses, Andrew Jackson Davis, J. Murray Spear, Charles Linton, Mrs. Lenore Piper, and Mrs. John H. Curran.

There has been much poetry written automatically, many books and articles with historical backgrounds, and extensive information about the nature of life after death. Some startling philosophies acceptable to numbers of people are based upon this source of abstract ideas.

"OAHSPE" as automatic writing

One of the most impressive volumes admittedly written through automatic writing is the "OAHSPE," a so-called new Bible. It was written by Dr. John Ballou Newbrough in 1880. This is a tremendously involved book, comprised of about 850 pages, covering the history of our planet, the universe, the human race, major religions, the world of the present, and coming events.

Dr. Newbrough wrote the entire book in one year. It is said that he was told inspirationally to purchase the then newly-invented typewriter, and to sit at it every morning without any attempt to use it himself, consciously. He was told that his fingers would be guided without effort or thought on his part. At the same time he was told that he should not read a word of what was written until the entire manuscript was completed. It is claimed that he did this without question, and the OAHSPE is the result. This man must have been a superman if he didn't sneak a look through all those hundreds of pages!

The "Patience Worth" control as automatic writing

The entire work of Mrs. John Curran, whose output was attributed to the control of "Patience Worth," was done by means of automatic writing, starting with a Ouija Board. The book called *The Case of Patience Worth*, by Walter Franklin Pierce, has a complete account of Mrs. Curran's experience with automatism and contains some of the most exquisite poetry and historically accurate fiction imaginable, all received automatically through the guidance of "Patience Worth."

There are many modern works, purportedly received through the automatic or inspirational channels. An inquiry in any occult book store will turn up some of these.

Other cases of books written by automatic writing

Many years ago, the British archaeologist and architect, Fredrick Bligh-Bond, published a book called *The Gate of Remembrance*. It is the story of Bligh-Bond's excavations at Glastonbury Abbey. In this work are included the automatic writings he received which gave precise directions and resulted in the success of the undertaking of excavating this famous ruin. It is fascinating reading and gives one much to ponder about the value and source of his information.

Although I do not recall the details fully, I do remember a very interesting report I read about one experience with automatic writing—one which had remarkable evidential results.

The principal was a minister's wife, and the story was substantiated and documented to such a degree that I am sure it must inevitably have found its way into the permanent records of some research group.

The lady in the account received, through automatic writing, a plea for help, purportedly from a spirit, earthbound because she had been buried on unconsecrated ground, part of the penalty she paid for her part in a murder. Details of the crime and subsequent punishment were given, including names, dates and locale.

Much mystified and disturbed by the story she had received, the principle wrote to the officials of the town where the events had been said to have occurred, a town outside the United States, as I recall. Subsequent correspondence established the truth of the details although the episode had taken place many years prior to the correspondence. Investigation showed that the messages were accurate on every count, including the location of the grave, conditions of burial, and other details. Full confirmation was made only after a long and painstaking probe because of the great lapse of time between the crime and the contact by the restless and unhappy spirit.

Another story, which unfolded because of the contact of a restless spirit, had as a principal a professional writer. During the course of typing material one day, the author seemed to lose control sporadically, and the conscious writing was interspersed with sentences which the woman had not consciously written. The mysterious interjections, not related to the story being typed, added up to an appeal that the writer contact a man whose name and address were given, along with information relating to the death of the named man's brother. The completed message made no sense to the woman through whom it was written.

Her curiosity piqued by the incident, she wrote to the man as requested and found that, not only did the man exist, but also he had been most concerned about the death of a brother who had died under questionable circumstances.

AUTHOR'S EXPERIENCE WITH AUTOMATIC WRITING

My own experience with automatic writing has not been so exciting.

I started to do automatic writing purely out of curiosity, not sure whether it would work for me. Within ten minutes of initiating the attempt, my pen started to move. The first three lines were practically illegible, although the last word looks like "realm" and the last words of the second line appear to be "in the afternoon."

As I continued to sit with my hand relaxed, the point of the pen resting on the paper lightly, the writing gained legibility and momentum. Before the end of the first experiment the writing was clear and legible, although it bore no resemblance to my own. Two days later I attempted it for the second time and, as the first, the writing was sprawled and indecipherable at the start but cleared up very quickly.

In the ensuing months I received many pages of writing, always in the same large, round-lettered form which first manifested; within a few days it completely lost its untidy look and became neat and readable. From that point on it retained its own peculiar letter formations and manner of slanting deeply downward on the pages.

At only one time during the period I was experimenting did the writing vary. The explanation given on that occasion was that Dr. William Marley, who theoretically was controlling my hand, was unable to be present at that time. The script of this particular message was small, precise, and beautiful. (My natural handwriting is quite small, but that is the only characteristic in common with the new script.)

The part of the automatic writing that really confounded me was the accuracy and details with which interruptions would be predicted.

Prediction accuracy of automatic writing

At the time of this attempt to discover how this particular "psychic power" manifested, I operated an antique shop. During the course of almost every business day I had much leisure time, so I would put a pad of paper on my desk, hold a pen or pencil poised on the paper, and then read a book in order to focus my attention on something other than the paper and pen. I never read what had been written until the cessation of the movement of the pen. Each time that the writing concluded by stating that an interruption would necessitate a break in the contact, the nature of the interruption would be given. Within a matter of minutes, if a visit from a friend, a telephone call, or a customer's arrival were predicted, that precise thing would occur.

This happened at least eight times.

It was startling to see such evidence of precognition, whether the source was my own subconscious or the spirit control it alleged itself to be.

I received much sage advice through this force which called itself "Dr. William Marley." If it was an alter-ego of my own, I have much more wisdom buried in me than I ever suspected. If it were spirit control, I certainly was fortunate to have attracted such a solicitous and perceptive one.

Many of the messages pertained to my physical condition and need of rest. Although I do not consciously concern myself with such matters, it is completely plausible that my subconscious mind would. Some of the writings contained warnings about a few of the people with whom I worked in the field of phenomena, and this, too, I could accept as a sort of "inner knowing."

But what about the precognitive things? Even if they were from within myself and this was just the channel through which they could be brought to the surface, the least I accomplished was proving to myself that precognition was latent within. It is still there sleeping if it were ever there, for it manifested most evidentially through the automatic writing.

Circumstances changed in my personal life and I did not pursue the practice of this kind of experiment. In the work I did do with it, "Dr. Marley" said that his purpose in doing his part was to produce a book ultimately. Some day I may resume this to see if it will take up where I stopped.

THE MANY FORMS OF AUTOMATIC WRITING

Automatic writing takes many forms. There are innumerable cases reported in which the handwriting is startlingly similar to, or exactly like, the handwriting of the controlling spirit during his lifetime. Obviously, the evidence of this depends upon the availability of writing samples of the supposed control during his physical lifetime.

It may be in English or a foreign language. It many times is in code. It may be in a long-dead language.

It may be upside down or with letters which are connected from right to left. One form of it uses letters formed backwards and must be held up to a mirror to be read. Only in rare instances is it perpendicular instead of horizontal, but I have seen such examples.

Sometimes there are breaks between the end of one word and the beginning of the next. Sometimes even punctuation is properly included. My own was one continuous string of letters without break until the edge of the sheet of paper was reached—sometimes the break would come in the middle of a letter and the next line would begin with the remainder of the incomplete letter. After the whole piece was completed, the pen would stop moving. I would go over it from the beginning and draw short dividing lines between the words and mark the end of each sentence. Sometimes, because of lack of punctuation, it was difficult to decipher the meaning—it often took longer to translate the message than it did to write it.

At one time, in some of my group work, I met a man whose wife could, while under hypnotic control, write automatically with both hands at one time. Each hand wrote rapidly and clearly on a subject entirely unrelated to the subject matter being written by the other. Her husband, a hypnotist, would induce trance, give a post-hypnotic suggestion that she would be able to do this without conscious volition but with ease, bring her out of the trance, and then sit back to watch it happen. The subjects upon which the writings were based were not a part of the suggestion—they were entirely beyond conscious selection. This woman was not normally ambidextrous.

Certainly there is a vast field of exploration and experimentation available with the use of hypnosis. Personally, I am averse to the tendency on the part of amateur hypnotists to use it freely, although much of interest has come from the ranks of the amateur but *well-trained* hypnotists. I feel, as stated elsewhere but it bears repeating, that only the disciplined researcher can evaluate the material received and only the properly qualified hypnotist can be sure that what he is getting by way of results from someone in trance has any real value. Unquestionably, the use of hypnosis should be limited to those qualified to conduct such tests. This excludes no one willing to study the proper techniques—it simply separates the serious worker from the "fun" group.

Two of my friends who tried automatic writing during the same period I did received not only different material but in a totally different way. One was done completely in symbols, some of which we could not translate, and the other received hers in a strange combination of tiny fine line drawings and words.

AUTOMATIC PAINTING AND DRAWING

There are numerous accounts of automatic paintings and drawings. I have had personal contact with only one person who produced such results. She is a lovely woman of my acquaintance who has a collection of the most exquisitely drawn pictures I have ever seen.

In the conscious state she has drawn sketches, done oil painting, and the most beautiful water colors of orchids I have seen anywhere. The pictures are done realistically and in great detail—*all* kinds of orchids—and when one considers the intricacies of the many varieties of this exotic flower, this in itself is an indication of real artistry.

The really startling pictures, however, are those which she has in a separate collection. These are the result of automatic drawing and they are pure fantasy—filled with symbols, technically superb and dramatically different from her own style. These are all done with crayons; the lines are precise and clean, and the colors blended with faultless artistry. The subject matter consists of substantially realistic subjects which are dreamlike because of the relationship they bear to each other in the whole rendition. It is clear that they are spiritually symbolic, and it is a real pleasure to study them.

These drawings were executed rapidly and without false strokes. They were done in such a way as to preclude the idea that they were done with any conscious end in view, as each one was drawn color by color; that is, all the yellow was put in, then all the blue, then all the red, and so on. During the drawing process it was virtually impossible to know in advance what the completed picture would be until at least three of the colors had been used. Once a certain color had been used, it was never again picked up during the work on that particular picture. The strokes were rapid and sure and there are no redrawn lines on any of the pictures despite the intricacy and detail of the finished piece.

These drawings are mostly combined forms of butterflies, flowers, birds and beautiful angel-like faces. Of special significance to believers in spiritual symbolism, there is no sign of an ear on any of the heads.

The drawings were done with incredible speed. They are exactly placed on the paper so that perfectly proportioned margins were always left on all four sides, regardless of the size of the paper used.

When the principal asked about control, an unusual hieroglyphic-like design was drawn into each picture from that point on. It was some time before my friend and her husband discovered that this peculiar little pattern was really a name. It is so exactly the same in form that it looks like a rubber stamp, except that it varies somewhat in size and is drawn in pencil.

Quite often there are human interest stories in newspapers about someone who has this gift, although the stories are usually given only local coverage. Our local paper had a story some months ago about a woman in a nearby town with the gift of automatic painting. The best sources of such stories, however, are the periodicals which are principally concerned with psychic matters.

Because of the skepticism with which such stories are greeted, I can understand why this particular psychic ability and other automatic manifestations are not discussed generally by the people who can demonstrate them. Who can blame them for taking credit rather than mockery when they produce something of beauty in this manner?

HOW TO ENGAGE IN AUTOMATISM

You have only to exercise patience and willingness in order to try your own hand at automatism. Since automatic writing is the simplest and most easily developed form of automatism, I would say that this is a good exercise to start exploring. You need only paper and a pencil, plus the appropriate mental state. Use fairly large sheets of paper and a soft-lead pencil. From this point on, you're on your own. If you are a nonconformist, as I am, other people's rules do not necessarily apply to you.

If you have no idea about how to go on from this point I will tell you how I do it. I do not say this is *the* way to do it—I simply offer this description of how it worked for me in case you are at a loss on how to begin; you may know or find a better way for you.

I started, following another's suggestion, by holding my entire arm and hand off the desk top. The only thing touching the surface of the desk was the piece of paper and the point of the pen (which I used in the beginning, then changed to pencil). I soon discarded this as much too tiresome. I assumed a normal writing position and found it more successful for two reasons—first, it was not so awkward and second, I could work without fatigue over a much longer period of time.

Then, also contrary to advice, I did not determine the time or duration of any sitting. I found that it was unnecessary, as the "control" would take care of that—very often finishing in a few minutes but occasionally continuing for almost half an hour at one time.

I found it most impractical to heed the admonition that one should always sit at the same hour each time. I found that I was most successful when I followed my own impulse, regardless of "clock time." Morning, noon or night, on any day or every day, when I had the real urge to try my hand, I followed the impulse. It was fine for me, so it may work for you.

It *is* absolutely necessary that you be physically comfortable while working at any type of development, so it is possible that you may prefer working with a planchette, which is a device similar to that used on the Ouija Board. In place of the window and pointer of the Ouija Board table, there is an opening through which a pencil is inserted. I have never used one of these carriers for a pencil, so I cannot personally attest to the satisfaction of this method.

In my experience it proved to be most satisfactory to read a book as I was doing the writing experiment, since this seemed to me to be a fairly sure way to eliminate conscious control and preguessing about the message put down on the paper.

AUTOMATIC SPEAKING

Automatic speaking is even harder to prove than the phases of writing, drawing, or painting. It no doubt occurs with much frequency but, because it leaves no concrete evidence, it is hard to prove. I suppose trance-speaking by mediums is the most usual way it manifests, but all of us, at some time or other, blurt out words involuntarily. Haven't you ever said, "I don't know why I said that. It just popped out"? It's just possible that this may often be a manifestation of automatism.

Of course, glossalallia, the "speaking in tongues," when it is genuine, must be classified as automatic speaking. It appears to be entirely without conscious mind direction.

The difference between inspired speakers and automatic (in the context to which we refer here) speakers is very difficult to determine by observation; even the speaker himself might have trouble trying to decide. It is much easier to accept the automatic concept of words we have written down without conscious volition when we can read them after we have put them on paper, than it is to believe that we *spoke* without forethought of the words we said. After all, unless we are in trance, we hear the words flowing even as we are saying them. However hard it may be to prove, I am sure that we all do automatic speaking at times.

Even though there is, at present, no provable explanation for it, you may find this phase of psychic ability very interesting and fruitful. Just remember—don't govern your life by the content of any of the messages, unless you can prove that the source, whatever it is, has your best interests at heart.

SUMMARY OF CHAPTER SEVEN

1. Automatism is variously attributed to disembodied entities and the subconscious mind.
2. Automatism manifests in many forms, such as writing, drawing, painting, and speaking.
3. Automatism is practiced without foreknowledge of the next word, stroke, etc.; inspirational work is done with awareness of what must be done next in order.
4. There are many fine works, both old and modern, acknowledged to have been produced through automatism.
5. Automatism can produce evidential information or ability which seems to preclude conscious or subconscious control.
6. Automatic writing may take many forms—backwards, upside down, perpendicular, childlike scrawls, or exquisitely formed script and languages (both foreign and ancient) unknown to the experimenter.
7. Drawings and paintings done automatically are frequently done with unbelievable speed and minute details.

EIGHT

Proof of

Reincarnation

with Psychism

Since the beginning of man's ability to record his ideas, even in the most primitive way, reincarnation has been alluded to as a part of his quest into the most unknown part of life. Reincarnation is still a widely embraced belief; in fact, it is considered by many religionists to be the closest thing to a common denominator in the world of spiritual thinking.

Although it has not enjoyed much popularity in the tenets of modern Christianity, it was nonetheless a part of the Christian Bible until the second Council of Constantinople, circa 543 A.D., at which time open references to reincarnation were deleted. The vote was two to three, a close decision, but all direct and obvious references to this concept were removed. Anyone teaching it thereafter was threatened with severe censure. Some of the early Christian teachers defied this edict; it was their contention that one could not understand Christianity if he did not understand reincarnation. This chapter will explore the credible bases of reincarnation.

BIBLE REFERENCES TO REINCARNATION

An open-minded search of the Holy Bible as we know it today will reveal to the serious researcher references to the concept of

113

rebirth: Matthew XVII:11–13; Mark VI:14–16; Luke IX:18–19; Luke XI:24–25; John III:13; John IX:1–3; John X:9; Revelations III:12, among others. Careful Bible study in the last 50 years has made the concept of reincarnation more acceptable to Western theology than in any comparable period of time since the revision took place.

The difference between reincarnation and transmigration

In order to clear up a popular misconception, let me here give an explanation of the difference between reincarnation and transmigration. It is surprising how many people confuse the two.

Both schools of thought teach rebirth, a succession of lifetimes on earth granted us to attempt to attain spiritual perfection. Transmigration is the earlier and is considered by many to be the more primitive, since it is the version which allows the soul to be embodied in any form of life, including insects and the lower animals, according to one's previous life-experience accomplishments or lack of them. This idea of rebirth is mostly an Oriental concept. Reincarnation teaches that man, once embodied in human form, continues his spiritual climb by being never less than human again. Almost every modern reincarnationist subscribes to the thought that man does not regress—he is constantly progressing, so it is this phase of the philosophy to which reference will be made here.

It is not my purpose to persuade anyone that reincarnation is the true answer. Lest anyone think I am going to evade a commitment of my own thought on this matter, let me say now that I find reincarnation a plausible and acceptable theory.

It is much too complex in its many facets to deal with here. There are some variations or interpretations of it which I do not find satisfactory to my own picture of it, but I should like to say that I do not find that it conflicts in any way with the teachings of Jesus.

Is reincarnation a proven reality?

Now we come to the question: "How can this theory be proven to be a reality?"

There is no area in one's life so difficult to explain and prove as in the things of spiritual conviction. Gautama the Buddha said, "Believe nothing because a wise man said it. Believe nothing because the belief is generally held. Believe nothing because it is written in ancient books. Believe nothing because it is said to be of divine origin. Believe nothing because someone else believes it. But believe only that you yourself judge to be true."

Up to this time I must admit that my acceptance of reincarnation has continued to satisfy me because it is based upon the appeal it has for my reason, even after much consideration and study. I could not prove its truth if my life depended upon it. Perhaps the field of psychism will find the way, given enough time and effort in intelligent experiments. Perhaps the most highly specialized researcher in the investigation of reincarnation is Dr. Ian Stevenson. During the course of his studies he has traveled thousands of miles and investigated cases all over the world.

Evaluating accounts of reincarnation

In evaluating information gleaned from a case of purported recall of a past incarnation, naturally the most important consideration is the amount of verifiable or evidential material which is forthcoming. It goes without saying that claims to having been an important historical figure whose life has been historically reported in the most minute detail for posterity would be almost impossible to evaluate. The sources of information are too numerous.

Frequently there are many interesting items revealed about a past lifetime, seemingly impossible for the subject to know in a more normal manner than recall of this sort. However, there must be at least six provable points brought out before it is advisable to waste time in tracking down the possibility.

If 15 or more coincidental items appear in the recall, a professional investigator will be interested. He will delve in, working on the case with three possible hypotheses in mind: normal acquisition of the knowledge about the deceased person (now believed to be incarnated in the subject being examined), paranormally derived knowledge without survival as a factor (thus allowing for the ESP faculty), or some form of survival or rebirth with recall of the past incarnation.

Since reincarnation has been a major part of the philosophy of the East for centuries, it is only natural that most of the stories of recall of past lives should come out of that part of the world. Children of the East who speak of memories of the distant past are not ridiculed or punished for having overactive imaginations. Children of the West are either disregarded by their parents when they relate such "stories" or are punished for lying. Fortunately there is a growing change of attitude on the part of many Occidentals, thus providing some opportunity to do investigative work closer to home than the Orient.

Case history analyses

Some time ago I knew of a child, three years old at the time, who talked of remembering being killed at a certain railroad crossing in the town where he lives. This child, far too young to demonstrate that much creative imagination accurately, has told of being unable to extricate himself from the engine of the train which struck him because of the fact that one of his legs was entangled in the "cow-catcher." It does not take a statistician to figure that this one detail of a cowcatcher on the front of a locomotive is descriptive of an engine obsolete for many years. Neither is it the type of descriptive item a child would have heard discussed in enough detail to make a lasting impression. To be sure, this is not conclusive, but it is intriguing.

The father of this child, a professional man, and the mother have handled this case with intelligence although they are at a loss to explain the child's story.

A few years ago I was told of another child, a boy of approximately the same age as the one mentioned above, who was also startling his family with stories of his death. He appeared to have full recall of his death in a war, and the facts that the child gave were historically correct as to dates and circumstances. This was certainly beyond the normal memory capacity of a child his age. My informant in this case made a conscientious effort to make it possible for this to be investigated further, but the child was never made available for study. The mother was understandably reluctant to expose him to what she felt might be an exhausting or upsetting inquisition.

It is not hard to sympathize with parents facing this dilemma, but a trained investigator knows how to handle this sort of thing with restraint and subtlety. There is much to be learned from such cases and anyone knowing of one would be doing a great favor to mankind if he would do all possible to persuade the family to contact a reliable researcher.

The investigation of possible recall by very young children is especially important since passing years expose all of us to such a great fund of information which might consciously be forgotten but which could greatly color the information given. The subconscious mind is the storehouse of every particle of data to which we have ever been exposed, regardless of the manner in which it was received by our senses. This greatly complicates the sifting of material, and whereas it does not render an accurate evaluation impossible, it certainly makes it more tedious and time consuming.

Granted that even a three-year-old can be very imaginative and inclined to exaggeration; nevertheless, it is easy to see that a child this young would not be capable of calculated fraud or drawing from the source of his own memory over a prolonged period of time with sustained accuracy. This is meant to be no implication that an adult necessarily resorts to fraud or conscious recollection if he appears to be recalling a past existence. I merely wish to make clear the point that research is much shorter and more conclusive if the evidence is forthcoming from the very young.

An argument for belief in reincarnation

It is my belief that one of the strong arguments for reincarnation is the differences in character, abilities and personality traits in children born of the same parents, subject to the same environmental influences and with the same cultural and financial atmosphere during their formative years. I feel that it can only be caused by the soul consciousness that is different because of past lives, thus reaction and response to the same stimuli are different.

For instance, I had to overcome a completely unexplainable fear of heights and water. These two common fears are not traceable to any event or influence in my childhood, and are not shared by any other member of my family. My brother is a talented artist and nobody else in the family can even approximate his ability, yet he had no training. My daughter is a very accomplished pianist in a long line of non-musicians. We all have a different outlook on life and are certainly individuals rather than copies of each other. There is some physical resemblance, but there the similarity ends.

To me this is only understandable if we each brought some thought patterns or abilities of our own with us. Experience is what makes us act and think as we do, and where it cannot be explained by environment, training or experiences in this life, there does not seem to be any other reasonable explanation for it. This of course does not constitute proof as we know it, but it has helped me to continue my belief in this concept. I do not feel that the genetic theory fills in as many gaps as reincarnation does.

Four avenues available for proof of reincarnation

Up to the present there are four ways that researchers are exploring the possibility of reincarnation: reverie, recall (which is much like the method described later as a meditative practice), mediumistic readings, and hypnotic regressions. These methods are used upon occasion by psychiatrists and psychologists in therapy sessions as there is some evidence that complexes and obsessions are alleviated or obliterated by the belief that the origin of the difficulty was in a previous existence. This possibility is entertained only by progressive practitioners, of course. Psychosomatic illnesses respond dramatically in some cases, and anxieties are often prevented from growing into tragedies by such sessions.

There has been much written about regression under the influence of hypnosis, but I cannot help wondering how much credence can be attached to the material received while the subject is under control. There is too much of a possibility range in the amount of influence exerted by the desire of the subject to please the hypnotist. It is true that there have been exciting reports and puzzling stories told by subjects under trance, but when one realizes that psychic perception can be very acute during the trance-state, there is much which must be taken into consideration when evaluating the results. It may be that this information may be coming from the subconscious, but it is also possible that it may be telepathically received by the subject from the mind of anyone within reach of his projected mind. It is not a question of intent to fabricate—it just seems to me that while under hypnosis a subject has access to information from sources too innumerable to calculate.

Although I have been trained in the induction and use of hypnosis, I personally do not approve of the use of hypnosis unless genuine benefits can be derived from each session. It is a wonderful therapy tool, but for the risks involved in its use in the depth of trance required for regression, I would want to be sure that a qualified person was in command if I were to be the subject.

I have had personal contact with three people who suffered severe emotional damage from ineptly conducted hypnotic sessions of the regression type. Two of them came to me to see if I could help them find relief from the severe nervous conditions which resulted from their experiences. The third person had finally achieved peace of mind, but only after many months of suffering.

Two of these people had been put through the horrible experience of reliving a past life experience of death by violence, one by fire, and the other by strangulation. In the latter instance, the subject was a woman. She had been regressed back to "a former incarnation," brought forward to her time of death, and allowed to go through traumatic horror of death at the hands of a man who strangled her. She came to see me about three and a half months after this experience. During the intervening months she had been hospitalized because she could not swallow, had required tranquilizers, and in other ways was in pretty sad condition. The severe throat disorder was no doubt psychosomatic but it was certainly unnecessary. The experiment proved nothing and the poor woman suffered physical and emotional torment needlessly.

Safest way to pursue existence of reincarnation

One of the safest ways to pursue the probing of pre-existence, if such a pursuit has appeal, is through self-analysis and meditation. We all have likes and dislikes for which we cannot reasonably account.

Just as an example—I have an unexplainably strong aversion to Oriental decor. This is not a family influence, as my brother once had his bedroom done in Chinese style, which would eliminate the family prejudice idea since my parents would not have indulged him in this if their feelings had been as biased as my own. I have always had a marked interest in Chinese history, but I wanted no more intimate contact than the written word. This is not a matter of taste—it is much more deep-rooted than that. I can appreciate the artistry of their work but I cannot be comfortable with it. When buying store stock for the antique shop I had to force myself to purchase anything Chinese.

Fortunately, I do not feel this way about Chinese people. I have learned to accept people as the individuals they are, not as part of the race, creed or group to which they belong. I feel that there is a strong likelihood that sometime in the distant past I had an unhappy or restrictive life in China. This has resulted in the strong feeling of revulsion when I am reminded of it.

Three years ago I was in a group which went to a nearby city for a visit with a famous medium. During the course of the evening, although I had said nothing about any fears or dislikes which had been part of my make-up, the medium told me that I had had to overcome a fear of both height and water. Her explanation was that I had, in a previous lifetime, been thrown from a high cliff into deep waters in a murder attempt. Here again we have an explanation of a complex, believable but startling because of the circumstance under which it had come forth. Certainly proof is sadly lacking. I can accept it as a perfectly feasible explanation; I can convince myself that the person who gave it to me is an excellent psychic; but there is still no *proof* that I actually lived that life.

The other members of the group were also told of past existences which were reasonable enough to be acceptable considering the personalities of the persons to whom they were told. Again there was no conclusive evidence that this was more than a demonstration of telepathy or character analysis. The medium was not fraudulent, certainly; this is not the question in my mind. There was plenty of proof of psychic ability, but there was nothing evidential to substantiate that these were really readings into past lives.

A common personal attitude toward reincarnation

Perhaps the attitude which causes most difficulty for researchers into the field of reincarnation is the reluctance of all of us to hear that we might possibly have lived lives as insignificant nobodies who made no great contribution to world history. Everyone would like to feel that he was a great personage whose name has gone down in history as a ruler, philosopher, artist, philanthropist or such, or at the very least a teacher of great magnitude.

No woman enjoys being told that she was at Versailles—as a scullery maid; no man wants to hear that he was active in Civil War days—as a weed-picking slave in a cotton patch. And yet such people did live and work up the evolutionary ladder, if reincarnation is a reality. Spiritual attainment does not always manifest in material position—it shows as character and spiritual strength. The world could not have progressed without the little people; each plays a necessary part in the whole picture. As far as I am concerned there is no such thing as an insignificant life, be it a scullery maid or queen, slave or master. One could not function in his position without the other.

What purpose would be served by knowledge of reincarnation?

A question frequently asked in almost any discussion of reincarnation is, "What good purpose would be served by having knowledge of reincarnation and past lives?" Here again we run into the differences in individual sets of values and truths. To some people it is of much importance and to others it does not matter one iota. Some say that it helps them to understand themselves and others better, as it gives some clue to reactions to given situations. Others seem to feel that they would have a better understanding of what it is that they lack in their struggle to finish their course of spiritual lessons. Still others are only interested in proving that reincarnation is the true answer to survival and the continued or eternal existence of the soul.

Since I believe that we are as we are and react as we do because of a series of past life experiences (at least in part), we should do everything possible to derive all possible benefit from the lessons learned to the extent that we can absorb them. Complete details are not necessary. However, since it also seems to me that it is only through recall of evidential details that the theory can be proven, I should like to contribute whatever I can by way of finding the way to prove it. I don't care *what* it is proven that I was a thousand years ago; I'd just like to prove that I *was*.

Although psychical researchers have not as yet come up with a way to prove reincarnation, they have certainly stimulated interest in it. During the course of pursuing their investigations many have embraced the concept themselves.

FAMOUS PEOPLE WHO ACCEPTED BELIEF OF REINCARNATION

The history of this school of thought is replete with famous names. Among some of the great people who accepted this belief were Pythagoras, Plato, Aristotle, Virgil, Ovid, St. Augustine, St. Francis of Assisi, St. Gregory, Schopenhauer, Voltaire, Nietzsche, Carlyle, Masefield, Walt Whitman, Ralph Waldo Emerson, Thomas Edison, Henry Ford, Flammarrion, Luther Burbank, Rudolph Steiner, Dr. Alexander Cannon and many others equally prominent and respected in the past and the present.

It is true that we should not believe simply because others believe, but the fact that we read such names as the above points out that this is not a theory which can be dismissed on the grounds that it is not acceptable to thinking people. It has satisfied more than the primitive and superstitious minds. It is not limited in its appeal to the weak in character who use it as a crutch or as a solace so that they may be able "to catch the brass ring on the next trip around, so why try now?"

THE MATERNAL IDEA OF REINCARNATION

There are many people who feel that they have lost children in death only to have them restored to them in the body of another child born to them a few years later. I have met several such mothers. The stories they told and their reasons for feeling that these were indeed cases of rebirth were not the irrational or hysterical voicing of grief; they were beautiful and believable accounts of exact duplications. For example, one child had been murdered and the other child had died of a tragic and painful illness. These women *knew* their children had been returned to them.

COMPATIBILITIES AND ANTAGONISMS

There are people who are unusually compatible in relationships such as marriage, friendship, family ties, teacher-student, and others, who feel that this closeness is the result of past-life associations. Inexplicable antagonisms may also be explained in the same way. We all have had the experience of having known someone before, even though we know we are meeting him for the first time. Some people never quite "win us over" in much the same way.

Even places can stir within us the feeling that we have been there before. The first day I was in the state of Massachusetts, I felt as if I knew one of the little towns as well as the town in which I have lived for over 30 years. I went off the main road and headed directly to an old, old shop just like a homing pigeon. *I knew somehow that shop would be right there.*

At one time or another we all have felt that some experience was one we have undergone before—and yet we "know better." These, I feel, are the stirrings of our deepest memories.

Since these things happen to us spontaneously, it seems reasonable to conjecture about the possibility of strengthening this ability just as one strengthens any other ability through disciplined practice. I wonder if the best way might not be to learn to "be still" and wait when we get these feelings. Perhaps we could learn to stay tuned in to the same wave length upon which the impression came initially.

MEDITATION AS RECALLING PAST LIFE

There is one recommended method of meditation which seems to have some promise of inducing recall. Although the instructions do not include any suggestion that true recall of previous incarnations might be the result, it is so similar to patterns used in other methods that it seems to me that recall might result if the regression were carried one step further. The procedure to which I refer is as follows:

Sit quietly, let your mind drift back over the events of the day and select the most pleasant and gratifying one, no matter how brief or insignificant. Then drift back through the past week and pick the most pleasing experience during that period. Then do the month in the same manner; then the year; then the life. It seems to me that anyone adept at this should be able to take the extra step and go into the immediate past life, since this state of mind is so similar to the level of consciousness used in regressive sessions for therapy. The conscious mind is quiescent and impressions can flow from the subconscious and the superconscious without difficulty. This does not bring us proof unless verifiable material is forthcoming, but it is a system of discipline which is suitable for solitary application away from the possible intrusion of the thoughts of other people.

EXPERIMENTS WITH PHYSICAL DEMONSTRATIONS

One interesting and simple experiment, believed by many to show past incarnations, is to sit with a group in darkness; use a red flashlight with a very dim bulb or else cover the lens of the light with red fabric—the light must be *very* dim but red. Have each sitter hold the flashlight under his chin in such a position as to eliminate as many of the shadows as possible—then watch for the changes which will transform his face. Sometimes the change is immediate, but it usually takes a little while—perhaps two or three minutes. Frequently the changes will be numerous, extreme and startling. They may vary from beautiful and delicate feminine features to coarse, ugly ones—all on the same person. It may be that only one change will take place, but it is interesting to note that all present see the same thing at the same time.

These changes are indicative of personalities expressed by the principal in past incarnations. It is certainly strange to see a lovely young woman become an ancient, heavy-featured Indian, or a strong masculine face turn into that of a fragile curly-haired child before your very eyes!

One evening some friends and I were doing this experiment, and we saw something which horrified all of us. One of the men was the principal at the moment. He was a square-jawed Germanic type. We were shocked to see his face become gaunt and agonized, one eye torn from its socket and resting on his cheek with blood streaming down that side of his face. In discussing this later he told us that he felt nothing definitive at the time this transformation took place, but he was not too surprised, since he had always felt that at one time he had been a pirate. None of us knew this, so we ruled out the power of suggestion from foreknowledge of this man's impression of his own past lives. Could it be that his conviction was so strong that he projected this image? Possibly. But this was not the face he imagined he had possessed as a pirate. Coincidence? That's certainly the easy explanation. (Remember what Gautama the Buddha said as quoted in the first part of this chapter?)

A mirror demonstration

Another experiment is similar in nature, but might be considered of less value since it is done alone in front of a mirror, and thus lacks the verification achieved through the simultaneous witnessing of others as in the previous method. Using either a candle or a small red light (as described in the previous experiment), stand in front of the mirror and look deeply into your own eyes. As you continue to watch unswervingly you will see a transformation take place. This will become very clear and sharp; it will appear to be the visage of a stranger, and yet you may have a strong feeling of kinship with the person portrayed in the mirror. Those who believe that this is a way of seeing yourself as you once were claim that this feeling of closeness is caused by recognition by your deepest consciousness of one of your own faces in a previous existence.

Experiments demand firm control over yourself

If you are easily frightened or upset, I strongly advise that you leave these foregoing two tests to others. I have known some who were dreadfully disturbed by images they have seen on themselves or on others. The mirror experiment especially is not for the faint-hearted. In the first one you at least have the comfort of company if the results are distressing.

A far-reaching demonstration mystics use

Finally, here is one variation of an exercise used by some mystics. It is very like self-hypnosis and may result in sleep, but there is no danger as long as you are faithful to the directions as given. As a prelude to any form of meditation, relaxation is a must. This can best be brought about by deep breathing exercises and by making yourself as comfortable as possible physically.

After you are as comfortable and relaxed as you can get, place your right hand over your solar plexus and the left index finger on your forehead in the "third eye" region—the center of the forehead above and between the eyes. Now think of your consciousness as a fine point of light in either your solar plexus or the crown of your head and *will* this light to spiral out and up, each circle widening as it goes out into space. As you *will* this spiral of consciousness to go farther out, think of a time period approximately 75 years in the past. (The older you are, the farther back into time you send your thought.) As you drift along with your consciousness projected, impressions will begin to occur. You may see people or events, hear conversations or participate in them; whatever impressions you get, make note of them the moment you end your meditation. As you progress in the achievement of this result, you may increase the number of years you send your consciousness back, preferably in cycles of about 75 years.

I have included these experiments here, not because they have *proven* anything to me, but because they appear to have given many people a great deal of inner satisfaction and self-command.

At this time, however, the question still remains in my mind— "Can psychism prove reincarnation?"

SUMMARY OF CHAPTER EIGHT

1. Reincarnation is the proper term for rebirth in human form or higher; transmigration is the concept that man may return as a lower form of life, such as an insect, animal, etc.
2. Cases of evidential recall of past lives are on the increase and are attracting the attention of more and more serious researchers.
3. It is becoming more acceptable to consider the possibility that childish "imagination" may sometimes be the spilling over of memories of past lives, close to the surface of the conscious mind.
4. Researchers into reincarnation use four methods of investigation: recall, reverie, akashic readings, and hypnotic regression.
5. The value of proof of past lives varies with individuals.
6. There are several different ways you may encourage your own "recall" experience with psychic methods described in this chapter.

NINE

Astral Projection:

Its Techniques

and Uses

Travel bureaus, transportation lines and space engineers may not have to worry about being obsolete within the next few years, but there is a remote possibility that they may be outmoded sometime in the future. I have nothing against any of these business and technical operations, but the prospect of such a situation presenting itself is not only exciting, it is entirely conceivable. By projecting yourself astrally, all it takes is practice and an iron nerve to develop the ability to go anywhere in the world (or, according to some reports, anywhere in the universe), instantly at will. No complicated timetables, no waiting for reservations, no scrimping to accumulate enough cash for a ticket, no bother with luggage! This chapter will tell how all this may be done.

HOW ASTRAL PROJECTION WORKS

The term "astral projection" is almost self-explanatory. It might be briefly described as the ability to send out from the body, at will, the spirit form which is our astral body. The astral body is an exact duplicate of the physical body, though so much less dense in form that it is invisible to normal sight. It is the carrier of our consciousness and responds to our thought instantly. It is this immediate response to thought which, as a rule, causes most novices in astral flight, while conscious, to be too frightened to attempt it again.

It is unfortunate that, as with so many other things, projection *methods* are sometimes learned before a thorough understanding of all facets of the accomplishment is attained. There are many who learn to project, then because they do not know how to cope with the experience, they are nearly frightened out of their wits and give up all further work with it. I know some people who have practiced projection and found it to be completely enjoyable because they know what to expect and how to control it.

Necessity of preliminary conditioning

Recently, a terrifying experience was undergone by a man who had been taught projection by a teacher who apparently was not qualified; no teacher worth his salt will instruct a pupil how to do projection before he teaches him what *not* to do, or at least gives him some idea of how to handle himself during the experience. This particular student, soaring around his home city looking at familiar sights, had a random thought—"How would it be to go to the moon?" Instantly he was hurtling through space at an unbelievable speed. His extreme fright caused his astral body to snap back into his physical body with shocking impact. This experience was so dismaying that he has never again tried to project himself astrally!

The term "learning" is really not appropriate when applied to simple astral projection, since this seems to be a natural and spontaneous occurrence, taking place to a degree each time we lose our normal state of consciousness, whether due to sleep, anaesthesia, or any alteration of the normal conscious state. The "learning" applies to projecting at *will* and retaining awareness during the experience.

THEORETICAL COMPOSITION OF ASTRAL BODY

The astral body is believed to be one of the many bodies man possesses, all of which are interpenetrating the physical body. Each body is of lesser density than the physical body, and death is no more than the permanent "leave-taking" of these bodies, taking with them the consciousness, intelligence, personality, memory, and emotional nature intact since they are the repositories for these faculties.

Spiritualists contend that each cell of the physical body has a vital, or psychic, center and that these millions of centers are what constitute the astral and etheric bodies. Since these cells are infinitely smaller than the cells of the physical, the astral body weighs only about an ounce and a half and, as a result, when the astral is released from the physical, it floats or soars upward. (This approximation of the astral body was determined in scientific tests of the difference in weight of the physical body recorded at the exact moment of death.)

THE "SILVER CORD" LINK

The astral generally hovers over the physical body while we sleep, connected by the "silver cord," which is the umbilical link between the astral and the physical bodies. If, or when, the silver cord is severed, death takes place. The spiritualistic concept is that we progressively shed our various bodies, each time functioning in a body of lesser density; what we call death is merely one of the discarding processes. When we reach the state of pure spirit, all of the bodies will have been discarded.

The silver cord connecting the bodies together is the "telephone line," and during a projection the physical body is protected by this communication to consciousness. A loud sound, the name being called, or any disquieting circumstance will recall the astral into the physical body, reanimating it.

Although we are not usually able to remember the events taking place when our physical body sleeps, our astral retains the consciousness, and during the sleep of anaesthesia, the astral hovers about, fully aware of what is transpiring and undistressed by it. Some theories pertaining to the relationship between the astral disengagement and anaesthesia are based upon the supposition that narcosis or anaesthesia renders the body incompatible or unsuitable for occupancy by the astral for a period of time determined by the amount of anaesthesia or narcosis rendered. There are many accounts, documented by the most careful researchers, of patients witnessing their own operations, watching the proceedings with great interest but with no physical sensibility. There have been accounts by doctors and nurses who have witnessed the separation of the bodies at death.

DREAMS AS BASED ON ASTRAL PROJECTION

Excursions taken by the astral body may account for some of the vivid dreams we have; possibly precognitive or premonitional dreams are in this category. If it is possible for the astral body to project, it is not inconceivable that two projected consciousnesses, having some common bond, could meet and converse about matters of interest. Perhaps the word "converse" is erroneous—"commune" would be more appropriate, I am sure, since the all-knowing mind is powerful in its concepts and words as we know them might be unnecessary.

EXPERIENCES IN ASTRAL PROJECTION

Some years ago I heard a man speak on the subject of out-of-the-body experiences, and he claimed that he had had many rendevous with friends and associates, each of whom had the ability to project at will. Although many miles might separate the physical bodies, they regularly met astrally by prearrangement!

Some of my friends have had spontaneous conscious projections. Several of them have said that they were very frightened when they found themselves hovering in space, looking down at their inert bodies. All of them, as the feeling of panic grew, were catapulted back into their physical bodies. This sudden re-entry of the astral into the physical is supposed to be the explanation for the violent start with which we sometimes come out of a state of sleep; something causes the re-entry process to be executed too quickly.

The sensation one feels as the astral leaves the physical while the consciousness is present has been described by those who have experienced it as varying from a lovely floating feeling to a horrible oozing effect. Those who have described it as a pleasing experience have been able to avoid the feeling of panic for a more prolonged period and have said that they felt the ability to project at will was worth cultivating. Each of those who enjoyed it, with two exceptions, had a fair understanding of astral projection before the conscious disunion took place. One of them, a woman, had developed the ability through will power, as an escape from pain, and did not know what was really happening. The other, a man, projected spontaneously and frequently as a child and retained his ability to do so until he lost interest—presumably this is the explanation, since he didn't seem to have difficulty with it long after he had reached manhood.

The woman who developed this ability as an escape from pain had a most interesting story to tell. She asked me one night if I could explain to her what was actually taking place. She was very puzzled by it but had not discussed it with anyone else because she was afraid she might be considered a little "peculiar."

It seems that she had been in an automobile accident serious enough to have resulted in fatalities. She had sustained critical injuries which required months of hospitalization followed by a long convalescence at home in bed. During the time of her stay in the hospital she had been receiving heavy sedation and was told that upon her release she would no doubt have to continue it for a prolonged period in order to relieve the intense pain which would accompany her convalescence. She said that the thought of continuing the intake of drugs, over the long period she had been told they might be necessary, frightened her. She decided that she was going to find a way to avoid taking sedation lest she become addicted. Although she knew nothing of astral projection, she felt that there must be a way to mentally rise away from her tormented body.

Lying in bed she would send her thoughts out into other parts of the room and into the corridor, willing relief from pain. She soon found that she could attain this relief from pain almost at will and found also that she could see other people and events in other rooms of the hospital.

After being taken home, where she still faced many painful months in bed, she said, she continued to practice this way of escaping from pain. Without understanding exactly what was happening, she found that she could see herself lying in bed but could feel herself soaring around the room at the same time.

It was now summer and she said that she found that she could escape the heat in her bedroom by floating herself out the window— by simply *willing* herself to be out in the coolness in her yard.

I explained astral projection to her, and told her what she had accomplished and what she could do with it. She was incredulous but agreed to prove it to herself by making some "test runs" to particular places where she would make note of details she could not possibly know, then check back for verification. Two such experiments convinced her that she was indeed projecting her consciousness, as both produced conclusive evidence of her phantom visits.

The man mentioned as having experiences in projecting as a boy is my brother. As a child, he would float out of his room into the living room and watch my parents play cribbage. As a man, during a very serious illness while in the service during World War II, he projected himself all over the hospital at Chanute Field. He familiarized himself with various sections of the hospital and some of the personnel in the offices, by taking reconnaissance flights during his many weeks as a patient. When he was finally allowed to be out of bed he found that he was thoroughly familiar with the hospital even though he was unconscious when he was admitted as a patient and had never been in the building prior to his admission. During the time of his illness he also made a few trips home to see the family, one time joining my parents on a fishing trip. So far as I know he has never had an unpleasant experience while accumulating his hours of "flying time."

Good reading on the subject of astral flights can be found in books by Hereward Carrington and Sylvan Muldoon. These two men did extensive research in the field of astral projection.

THE SPIRITUALIST THEORY

Although there is a possibility that this is only believed by spiritualists, it seems to me that it bears mentioning that, in order to avoid extremely unpleasant contacts during a projection, one must be sure that he is free from negative mental and emotional conditions before he attempts exteriorization. The spiritualist theory holds that in astral form one contacts all sorts of evil or malefic beings if the level of consciousness is not sufficiently high to ward off such contacts—again a reminder of the law that like attracts like. It is not unreasonable to assume that this may be so. If one should be projecting for any negative purpose it is feasible that negative forces would be attracted to the projected body. Astral is visible to astral, and the astral body of one being shows clearly the character, intent and weakness, or strength, it possesses to all other astral beings.

A hypothetical case

Let us take a hypothetical case: A man, in a bitter, vengeful state of mind, determines to project himself into the home of the object of his resentment, for instance, the home of his former wife, now happily married to someone else. He wants to attempt to "get even" in some way, and his sole thought at the time he sends himself on his astral journey is to do as much harm as he possibly can. This ugliness colors his astral body to the extent that anyone reading his aura (see chapters on auras) could see the menacing character of his thoughts, but it is even more clearly recognized by other beings in the astral state.

Speaking from the spiritualists' viewpoint, discarnate entities, whose nature might be as mean and vindictive, are attracted by the mood this man is aurally clearly showing in his astral form, and may join him to receive a vicarious satisfaction from accompanying him on his flight; in other words, he may find himself with a most unpleasant entourage or "gang" made up of entities that even he would prefer not to have attached to him.

It is also possible, according to spiritualistic concepts, that the object of his revenge might possibly be guarded by highly evolved spirit helpers who would give him a hard time when he arrived on the scene. Add to this the thought that during his astral absence his body might be claimed by an entity which was attracted by the low state of consciousness manifested by the projector before he left his body. It is claimed by some research records that it is possible for an invading entity to enter a body and put up a real battle to retain it when the rightful occupant returns. Possession is the result of such an instance.

These ideas are interesting and there is, in almost any collection of accounts of astral projections, information which would tend to make these theories worthy of serious consideration.

HAUNTINGS OF HOUSES AS ASTRAL PROJECTION

There are also some thoughts to the effect that not all haunted houses are frequented by ghosts, but that the astral form of someone who loved the house, or had some reason for returning to it, is really the "culprit." The longing or motive for returning to the scene may be so great that the astral is drawn back during sleep or sent back deliberately in a conscious projection. Considering the close kinship between astral projection and bi-location, this, too, is a reasonable theory.

BI-LOCATION PHENOMENA

Bi-location, for the benefit of those to whom the term is unfamiliar, is the ability to be (seemingly) in two places at once. In every case of bi-location of which I have ever heard, one's physical body appears to be in a deep sleep, trance or coma, while the projected body, to all intents and purposes, can be seen, heard and participate in physical activities in a perfectly normal way, in the eyes of the witnesses. The major difference between projection and bi-location apparently is a difference in density of the "projected" body.

Some of the cases of apparitions appearing to someone dear to them at a time of crisis are really bi-location, I feel, although there will no doubt be many who will disagree with me. The mastery of bi-location is one of the accomplishments of some Eastern adepts; one of the orthodox Popes was said to be able to bi-locate at will; and there are a few cases of spontaneous bi-location verified in modern psychical research records and publications.

An experience in bi-location

Following is an experience in bi-location which, because I knew the principal, I found especially interesting and believable. This person had gone into the city to shop. She suddenly felt exhausted and decided to go into a department store lounge to rest while her companion shopped. After a deep sleep for about a half hour, she woke, finished shopping and went home.

Her apartment was in the rear of a small neighborhood grocery store which she and her husband owned. When she arrived her husband was in a tearing rage. He furiously demanded an explanation of her behavior: what did she have by way of a reasonably passable excuse for going out a second time without a word of explanation? Further, what possible reason did she have for not speaking either to him or the customer in the store when she walked in and out?

The poor woman was completely bewildered by his tirade and could not understand what he was raving about until he simmered down a bit. It seems that while she was sleeping in the downtown store lounge, her husband and a woman customer saw her come into the store, walk through to the apartment in the rear, then walk back through the store and out the door without so much as a word. Not only did her husband and the woman customer *see* her, they both spoke to her and received no response. She had a hard time convincing her husband that she had not been there in the flesh; only the fact that he had some knowledge of psychical phenomena made it easier for her to explain the situation.

"Invisible" projection

It would seem that there is also an in-between state, where the projected body is not visible to the physical eyesight, but yet can make its presence known. I know one woman who had two such experiences. Each time her mother was the person made aware of her presence, once by touch and once by sound. In each instance the mother somehow knew that her daughter was involved in the experiences even though she could not see her.

In one of the episodes the daughter engaged in a severe argument with her mother while angry over something her mother had done unfairly—this in a dreamlike state when an ocean separated them physically. On the other occasion the daughter visited her mother's home and looked over some of her own prized possessions which her mother was keeping for her while she was away. Her mother was aware of the sounds during the second visit.

Both times each assumed they had been dreaming until they exchanged letters after the mother wrote describing the events she had "dreamed," explaining that, although of course they *had* to be dreams, she felt that she had been wide awake at the time the incidents occurred.

HOW TO DEVELOP YOUR POWER OF ASTRAL PROJECTION

There are many methods of developing the power of conscious astral projection. Anyone who would like to try astral travel must persist in his efforts in the way which seems most effective for him. I will give here some of the methods of which I know, some of which are effective for some and some effective for others.

Warning

Before detailing the methods, I feel that a few words of caution are in order. The reasons for proper motivation have already been dealt with, but a reminder would not be remiss. DON'T AT-TEMPT A PROJECTION FOR A NEGATIVE PURPOSE.

Another important point to keep in mind is that most researchers agree that no one with heart trouble should ever work to develop conscious projection. It seems that respiration alters considerably during a projection outside the normal cord-activity range, and this could create some difficulty in a heart patient. The normal spontaneous projection, unencouraged by effort, will only be in the framework of a safe range.

Finally, remember that to think is to *be*—if you are not capable of mind discipline, don't experiment with a state in which mind is practically all you are. Always bear in mind that in the projected state you go where you *think* you would like to be, are involved in situations you *think* you would like to experience, and *attract* to yourself consciousnesses of the same nature. *Don't invite traumatic adventures by careless thinking.*

Preliminary steps

All of the recommended methods of preparing for astral flights have a few features in common. As a beginning, rhythmic breathing is almost always suggested. This is the process of breathing in deeply for a count of eight or more, holding the breath for a count of eight or more, exhaling to the count of eight or more, and then immediately inhaling again. The count may be gradually increased in a comfortable manner until the respiration is as slow as possible without ill effect. Of course, you use the same count for inhaling, exhaling and the hold—if you start with eight, use eight on all three actions, and increase on all three as you can increase on any. Breathing in this manner is conducive to relaxation, which is another of the common features.

Relaxation is necessary on both the physical and the mental levels. The body must be free from tension, and the mind must be quiet enough to be capable of complete concentration.

Another of the common requirements is the development of the ability to prevent the normal sleep state from taking over the consciousness. If sleep comes fully, it is highly improbable that there will be any awareness or ability to recall a projection experience if it does take place.

The final common requirement is determination, or a very strong *will* to succeed.

Relaxation necessary

One of the most delightful ways to attempt conscious astral travel is so relaxing that the most difficult part of it is to prevent sleep from occurring. After the preliminary deep breathing and relaxing as much as possible, visualize yourself standing on a mountaintop on a clear night. Picture the sky bright with stars, clouds drifting lazily along between you and the earth below—as if you had risen above all earthly problems and worries. As you are standing there, think of all the things in your life for which you are grateful—think of them with gratitude in your heart.

After you have finished this careful inventory, mentally picture yourself making your way slowly down the mountain-side to your home, picturing in your mind as you go the place you wish to visit on your astral trip. Think of this as a trip you know you are going to take and are looking forward to with much pleasure.

Mental preparation

Mentally go through the motions of getting ready to go: dressing, getting into your car, starting on your way. *Feel* yourself getting underway, anticipating a safe trip, thinking with pleasure of your destination, and the person or persons you are going to see.

(If you begin to actually feel a floating sensation or motion, just let it continue, but tell yourself that you are going to retain consciousness of the adventure, knowing everything that takes place.)

Drive along in a leisurely way in your imagination, seeing the countryside as clearly as you can. Take your time in all of the steps—don't rush yourself. You will arrive at your destination while still in the fully awake stage if you hurry. The astral body is no longer under your conscious control if you fall asleep. It is necessary that you control the consciousness level in the in-between state of wide-awake and asleep, and this control cannot be rushed.

Try this exercise every night upon retiring, or at any time you wish during the day; astral flights do not take place at night only.

Voluntary effort

Another method which appears to be successful for people of strong will is to do just that—*will* yourself out. This method requires the same preliminaries of breathing exercises and relaxation, but then the picture changes. Visualize your astral body as a cloudlike replica of your physical body; imagine it as starting to float gradually upward, then *will* it to continue to rise. Persist determinedly in forcing it to emerge, parallel to your body and attached to the physical body by the cord. I know of one man who was successful in his attempt, using this method, after only one week of practice.

The fractional method

A third method of procedure is fractional. Close your eyes after the preliminaries are over, concentrate your attention on a segment of your body—your left leg, for example. While thinking of your leg, *will* the astral leg to emerge slightly. Concentrate on that leg until you feel it move out; then concentrate on the other leg, willing it to move out also. Work over the entire body in this way, *willing* the astral parts to move slightly out of coincidence with their physical places. Work over the entire body in this way, willing each section to displace itself at your command. Do not try to rush the procedure; use patience and persistence. It may take several attempts before you succeed even with the first segment. As you work, be sure that at the conclusion of the attempt you order the astral counterparts to go back into the proper normal position. After you know you have succeeded with the fractional projection, you are ready to project your entire astral body into space.

Group experiment

Although there are countless methods of inducing an astral projection, I shall include here only one more—group experimentation in which I participate that has produced favorable results. One was done, however, in unusual circumstances and results took place very quickly. It took place during a seance with a medium and five other sitters.

The seance had been in progress for about an hour, under the mediumship-guidance of a young spiritualist minister who demonstrated many facets of psychic ability. At this particular point, while being given a demonstration of trumpet communication, the voice speaking to us asked if we would like to experience an out-of-the-body projection, brief but real. The voice then instructed us to sit erect in our chairs with our feet flat on the floor and as relaxed as possible, physically and mentally.

We were then told to breathe in unison with a count which was given: "In, two, three; Hold, two, three; Out, two, three; In, two, three; Hold, two, three," and so on for perhaps five full rounds of the slow count and deep breathing. Then the voice told us to picture ourselves rising slowly out of our chairs, still in the sitting position, rising until we were entirely free from our physical bodies.

As the voice gave instructions in a slow, calm tone, I had the definite feeling that I was sitting on air, at least two feet above myself. We were then told that we should think of something we would like to see or a place we would like to visit. Just as I started to think of going out somewhere to look around we were called back to integration with the physical. Nevertheless, just before being "put back together," I found myself looking at a lovely walnut table with four exquisite red roses laid on the shining surface. There was something unusual about the flowers which did not register with me until later when I was thinking about the experience. I have no idea where I was nor why, but I did realize that the unusual look and position of the roses was because they were made from wax.

When we discussed our reactions later, one of the women said that she had visited a city which she did not recognize. She seemed to be looking at it from above and did not get oriented in time to determine where she was. It may have been an unfamiliar city which caught her attention while she was en route to her destination, and the experiment was concluded before she arrived at the place she had hoped to visit.

GENERAL GUIDES FOR PROJECTION

Preoccupation with projection seems to be a factor in bringing about success. Carrington and Muldoon both expressed the opinion that continued fear of the experience can bring it about as quickly as continued desire for it. Any mental activity employing the imagination seems to be an incentive or stimulus to the subconscious, whether the imagination is functioning fearfully or hopefully.

Anyone may work for astral projection using the methods suggested here, or some of the many others in print elsewhere, with the expectation of achieving success. Results are usually attained best at night, simply because that is the time the physical body is most apt to be depleted, and the livelier the body the less distance the astral goes out of coincidence. Physical incapacity, such as the state of almost cataleptic inertia which is in effect when in the very drowsy state immediately before losing consciousness in sleep, or just before returning to full consciousness when waking, is necessary.

Never make an attempt to move physically while inducing an exteriorization—it will not harm you, but it will draw the astral back into the physical and you will be defeating yourself in your attempt to project.

There is always a dimming of consciousness as the separation occurs, but it is only temporary if you learn to control this and can prevent yourself from slipping into sleep.

If you have a particularly vivid dream involving another person, check with that person if possible. It may be that it wasn't a dream after all but a meeting on the astral level. Maybe he will remember his, maybe not. It could be that just hearing about your experience will recall to his mind the "dream" that he had forgotten. I have heard of several dreams that turned out to be projections—both persons telling the same story in much detail and each aware that they had shared an expedition into another dimension.

SUMMARY OF CHAPTER NINE

1. Astral projection is a natural and constantly repeated event for everyone; recall of the experience is comparatively rare.
2. Astral bodies always exteriorize during sleep, faintings, anaesthesia, or any other form of unconsciousness.
3. Death is the permanent detachment of the astral from the physical; it results from severance of the "silver cord."
4. Exteriorization is usually spontaneous but may be deliberately brought about with full recall.
5. It is wise to induce projection only for good reason, since the law that "like attracts like" will determine the kind of experience you will have when "out of the body."
6. Bi-location is similar to astral projection, but the projected body is more dense and is visible to witnesses who may be miles distant from the supposedly sleeping principal.
7. There are several methods in this chapter for inducing projection with recall.

TEN

The Value of

Ouija Boards in

Psychic Development

A Ouija board is defined as, "Trade name for a board inscribed with the alphabet and other characters and equipped with a planchette, the pointer of which is thought to spell out mediumistic communications." Following the definition is given the derivation of the name: "oui" from the French for yes, and "ja" from the German for yes.

It seems unlikely that a Ouija board is an unfamiliar instrument to anyone who would be interested in a book of this nature, although there may be many who have not personally "worked" on one. I do not recall ever having seen any information in print on the origin of the Ouija, but I believe they were first sold in the form we know them around the turn of the century. They enjoyed great popularity at the time of World War I and then seemed to be relegated to closets to gather dust. In the past few years they have come into their own again, and this chapter discusses basic uses of this psychic mechanism.

USE OF OUIJA BOARDS NOT BASICALLY DANGEROUS

Although the use of the Ouija board is frowned on by many practitioners of psychism on the grounds that it can be dangerous, I feel that I must include it in this book. I feel that *anything* psychic in the hands of an unstable person may be dangerous, and *anything* uncontrolled or used immoderately is dangerous even in the hands of the otherwise stable-minded person. Since I have never had personal encounters with anyone who suffered ill effects from experimenting with this instrument, I feel justified including it in this book.

It cannot be stressed often enough that understanding and proper attitude on the part of a participant in any phase of development of psychic abilities is very important. It is my contention that there is no phase of psychism which should be labeled dangerous. It is ignorance and misuse that are dangerous. To say that a Ouija board is dangerous and an open invitation to evil is rubbish as far as I can see. Emotional instability can be dangerous if one is handling a gun, a glass of any kind, a table knife, medicine, an automobile or even a feather pillow. The danger lies in the untrained or thoughtless usage to which an object is put—not in the object itself.

One of the interesting points I have noticed about arguments against the use of the Ouija board is that the people propounding such warnings usually suggest some other form of automatism or mediumship as a substitute. If the Ouija is unsafe, so are all of the rest of them.

Anyone who looks upon a Ouija board as a dangerous or evil thing has no business trying to use it; and if he fears or believes that no good can come of it he ought to leave it alone and allow his less superstitious and more stable brothers to avail themselves of its performances. Like does attract like, and evil will come when it is expected; it will always respond to the call of fear.

Because of the extreme importance of the proper understanding and positive attitude on the part of a partner at a Ouija board, I never sit at a board with anyone whose character or knowledge of psychic work I have any reason to question. In my files I have a large loose-leaf notebook filled with letter-by-letter messages received during sessions with a few select partners. We have never had any unpleasant or vulgar manifestations in many years of experimenting and testing Ouija boards. Some of the material received has been the most beautifully worded philosophy I have ever read, some has been intriguing, and some of it amusing. I have no idea of the true source, but we have been given names and information indicating that it is spirit control. Despite this I will repeat that I *do not know the source personally*. I can only say that whatever it is it can only be good, because that is the nature of the material received.

I might also add that during these experiments we rarely asked personal questions. We simply waited expectantly for good to come and that is what we received. After the planchette started moving we would ask questions, but these were mostly in regard to the material being spelled out. If we had expected or feared evil, vulgarity or bad taste expressed in any way, I am sure that is what would have been spelled out.

There have been published in numerous books and periodicals many articles presenting material received by individuals and partners during board sessions. Much of it is good. There have been many unpublished stories told to me by people whose integrity and good sense I respect, which make me even more certain that just as beauty is in the eye of the beholder, so are evil and fear and ugliness in the mind of the superstitious.

Things have only those qualities with which we ourselves endow them. I know of no one personally who asks a Ouija board for advice as to how he should conduct his affairs, hence I know of no one who has been led astray by its influence. Any bad effects suffered as a result of such experiments with the board I know of only by hearsay, always prefaced by those maddeningly untraceable terms, "they" or "someone." It is usually, "someone I know told me about a person he knew" who suffered dire results, with no evaluation or reference to the stability of the "person" before the catastrophic experience took place. I have never been given proof that a Ouija board had really claimed another victim. It's like placing the moral responsibility for murder on the gun rather than on the person who pulls the trigger.

REPORTS ON OUIJA MESSAGES

One of my closest friends and I decided many years ago that we would work with a Ouija board to see if we could decide for ourselves the source of information we might receive thereby. Although we never arrived at any conclusion as to source, I must say that we spent many interesting and informative hours holding sessions.

There were a number of curious and thought-provoking aspects aside from the message content. For example, always preceding a "contact" by a certain force identified by the name of "Dr. Moloy," I would begin to yawn, the yawns increasing in frequency and intensity until my eyes and nose would run profusely. My friend always felt a pressure on her arms around the elbow area before a force which identified itself as "Dr. Melbeman" would begin spelling out words.

There were certain peculiarities which we came to recognize as indications of change of control and identifiable with frequent "visitors." For example, the planchette would move with much effort, as if weighed down by great pressure in the center; there would be free-flowing graceful movement, rapid and smooth; there would be short, choppy angular dartings; there would be much hesitance and uncertainty as if not sure of spelling; each control manifesting characteristics of its own strongly enough that a change of control was obvious even before we were informed by the spelling that a new force was taking over.

Precluding conscious control

In order to preclude any conscious control, at least, I usually kept up a continuous line of conversation while the letters were pointed out. Each letter was noted down as received and the whole series of letters was never separated into a message until the planchette stopped moving. We always made it a rule that no observer could tell us anything about what the message was until it had been received in its entirety, thus also providing a further obstacle to conscious influence.

Upon rare occasions we would get a few lines of completely garbled letters. We never thought to ask the board for any explanation of this performance; however, I was recently in a gathering where the Ouija board, as a psychical instrument, was under discussion. This confused activity was explained as a result of two or more spirits trying to communicate at the same time. If the board *is* activated by the control of disembodied entities, this explanation is reasonable.

Although there are many psychics who insist there are certain rules and regulations to which one must strictly adhere while functioning in the area of ESP, I am a nonconformist to the degree that I am willing to try it their way, but if it proves not to be as satisfactory or productive of the desired results I have found can be obtained, I am going to work under my own conditions.

Environment conditions

I don't go along with the theory that one *must* work a Ouija in a dimly lighted room, as some declare. I have sat in every conceivable kind of light, including red light, broad daylight, moonlight, blue light, no light (which we did once to convince a hardened skeptic that it is impossible to receive messages intelligently when one cannot see the letters as they are pointed out—some people are *very* hard to convince). We proved for ourselves that it makes absolutely no difference what the lighting conditions are.

One of the suggested requirements was wooden chairs. I have heard it said that it is impossible to obtain any results if you sit on metal seats. This, too, is an unnecessary stipulation as far as I can see, since I have sat on everything from the bare ground to a foam pillow. Whether the board is resting on the sitters' knees or a table top does not seem to matter either, although purely as a matter of preference I lean to the knee position.

"Dead" boards

There have been times when a board would appear to be "dead," sometimes even during sessions with my most successful partners. I do not pretend to know the reason for this, although I presume it was the result of incompatibility of vibrations at those particular times. Also I have had the experience of "dead" boards with certain people. This was explained as a question of wrong polarity, a condition which would be more or less permanent as far as the particular combination was concerned.

Best conditions

My favorite modus operandi, or method, is to sit in a comfortable armless chair (for freedom of arm movement) in a comfortably temperate or cool room with restful light conditions—in short, as comfortably situated as possible. Unless there is a third party present to note down the letters as pointed out, we usually note them down on a nearby pad in proper sequence as they are received, usually about three letters at one jotting, since it is very possible to forget the proper sequence of more than three if you follow our practice of not translating the message until it is completed.

RECORDING MESSAGES

One evening a friend and I decided that we would be very clever and call out the letters into the microphone of a tape recorder as they came. When we played it back for transcribing, we realized that we had made our work much more difficult, for the sound of so many of the letters is so similar that we could hardly tell the b's from the c's, p's, d's, e's, t's, etc. We found that notings with pencil and paper were much more satisfactory.

Here is a message received during a session and I shall show how the message appears before it is translated: Sciencepriesopen-manydoorsbuttoomanylookthroughthecrackwithunseeingeyestruthis bestseenwijusticeandwisdomwithopeneyes. This, of course, becomes intelligible only after words are separated and punctuation is done. We translated it as follows: Science pries open many doors, but too many look through the crack with unseeing eyes. Truth is best seen with justice, and wisdom with open eyes.

Most of the rest of the material in this chapter will be literal and exact transcripts of messages received while I was sitting at the board with one friend or another. They are exactly as they were received except that they have been "translated" for easy reading. When names were given for controls, they have been included, along with dates where noted and the initials of the sitters.

June 13, 1961, F. & H.:

Q. Is anyone here? A. Yes.
Q. Will you give us your name, please? A. Plarramom (this was a name familiar to us from past sittings).
Q. Where have you been? A. Manomoyokr.
Q. We don't understand that. A. Moments of maybe long time to you are passing fast to us.
Q. What does this mean? A. A very long absence to you is fleeting to me.

Q. You don't sound very friendly tonight. Is something wrong? **A.** I merely meant my hard work makes my time without seeing you shorter for me than for you.

Q. Please don't drain Harriet so much tonight. Would white lights or music help you instead of drawing so much from her? **A.** I am not draining her. She is being conditioned.

Q. We do not want any harm to come to her. Can we depend on you to see that this does not happen? **A.** I will guard her well.

Q. How do we know that you are not conditioning her for some selfish reason of your own? **A.** Evils such as that could not get through her light.

Q. How long is this conditioning period? **A.** I do not know.

Q. Why are you so slow tonight? **A.** Speed is not relative to wisdom.

(After an exchange with another "force" the control which called itself "Plarramom" came back.)

Q. Are you here, Plarramom? **A.** Yes.

Q. Do you have something to tell us? **A.** Sometimes when I collect thoughts I do not move very fast because I have a problem with words.

The message following pertained to a young man named "Lolly," about whom much more will be said later.

Q. We talked with Lolly after you left. We hope we were able to make him understand that he is in spirit. When he reaches the right level of understanding will you help him? **A.** I know you know I will. I will always help when I can.

Q. Were you close by when Lolly came? **A.** Yes.

Q. Did you see him? **A.** Yes.

Q. Will it be long before he understands what we were telling him? **A.** He is asking for help and that is good.

Q. We have to stop now. Please come again soon. Would you like to leave a message with us? **A.** Try to spread light and you will find your own path fully lighted.

Excerpt, July 1, 1961, F. & H.:

Q. Is anybody here? **A.** Yes.

Q. Will you give us your name please? **A.** Dr. Moloy.

Q. Why did you follow us out here? (We were at a friend's house for the evening.) **A.** I followed to give you this message. There is no night so dark that God's love cannot light it, no burden so heavy that His strength will not ease and no error so grave that His grace cannot forgive.

Excerpt, July 4, 1961, F. & H.:

The name Dr. Moloy had been given at the beginning. The message was as follows:

Friends must learn that the exchange of ideas without maliciousness or selfishness is one of the most valuable aspects of friendship.

Many learn the least the long easy way, few learn the short way, fewer still who cannot learn at all as God's time is eternity and His teaching methods equally limitless.

Excerpt, July 7, 1961, F. & H.:

Name of Plarramon had been given at the beginning:

Q. Are you still disgruntled with the world as you were the last time you were here? A. I feel very sad and many times angry at the selfishness and greed mortals show in their relationships one to another, but I love humanity as a whole and hope God's light will lift it out of the morass it has created.

Excerpt, July 11, 1961, F. &. H.:

The name, Dr. Moloy, had been given at the beginning.

Q. Before we say goodnight may we have a message? A. Let your light so shine that those who are still in the dark may see more clearly the path you already traveled and the path ahead of you will become more brightly lighted for you.

Excerpt, July 15, 1961, F. & H.:

These are the closing remarks after a dissertation on the progress made by new arrivals and the help available to them (in response to a question from us):

Help is given only where the level of consciousness permits penetration of new thoughts and concepts. Transition does not automatically bring wisdom nor broaden narrow minds.

Excerpt, August 23, 1967, F. & H. (Opening message by "Dr. Moloy"):

Strength of spirit brings with it all other attributes in proportionate degrees. If you would enrich your life with all good things, devote your major effort to understanding and developing your spiritual attributes and all other things must benefit by God's law in return.

Excerpt, September 24, 1967, F. & H.:

Q. Who is here tonight? A. Dr. Moloy.

Q. What do you have to tell us? A. Have more faith in Him who guides you every instant. He is the essence of good in each thought, word and deed in every man. As spirit He is here ever and always.

Q. Does this remark pertain to our conversation about the Ouija board? A. Yes.

Q. Are we receiving messages through controlled consciousness?

A. Yes. I am impressing your superconsciousness with thought and so am in effect in control.

Q. You mean someone is actually speaking to us through the board from a higher vibration? This is not information from the storehouse of our own subconsciousness? A. Much may seem familiar. These ideas may seem so because they come as recalled from the soul consciousness of your experiences. Some thoughts are new to you and come under the control of those of us who are helping you learn.

Q. Who has us in control when we are contacting supposed space people? A. Lessons must be learned by all who are growing. You are trying to learn to discern for yourselves the true spirit of your contacts. You will be safe from maliciousness but mischief will help develop discrimination.

Q. Why should we accept what you say, Dr. Moloy, and be leery about accepting anything from "space people"? A. There is no reason to accept me or anyone if your heart rejects. No one should take anything he is reluctant to absorb as his own good. There is no more accurate measure of merit for matters of spirit than that spiritual stature which you have attained and which manifests as faith and acceptance.

Q. Metaphysics teaches that there is no such thing as evil. This being so why does every living thing in nature have both a negative and a positive force? A. The negative and the positive are not meant to attract and repel but to attract and radiate that good which has been aquired by the attracting force.

Q. Metaphysics teaches that there is no evil. Why does the Lord's Prayer contain the line "Deliver us from evil"? A. Evil is merely a word symbolic of less than whole good. In reality all things contain good. It is only a matter of degree or proportion.

Q. What do you call that which renders good less good? A. Error.

Q. Will we have to evolve more before we will understand? A. Most of the understanding is yours already. It is stirring in its dormancy or you would not think to ask.

Excerpt, December 1, 1961, F. & H. Two or three new names were introduced in this sitting and when the name "Dr. Moloy" finally came we asked:

Q. Why did these new ones come? **A.** They will come to you in the future more frequently than anyone else other than Melbeman and I, as we will be with you permanently and others will come and serve or be served and then move on.

Q. Where is Plarramom? **A.** He has moved into the physical plane to fulfill a mission.

Q. Does this mean that he has been reincarnated? **A.** Yes.

Q. Can you tell us where? **A.** I can only reveal that his role will be of great import to world events in about 40 years.

Q. Will he return as a prophet? **A.** He will be a great teacher and leader under the greatest teacher and leader of the Aquarean Age.

Excerpt, December 6, 1961, F. &. H. During this sitting, one of the new names, "Bernardo Paoli," presented itself and closed with this message:

Every day means a new facet on the jewel that is life. Be sure that each new facet is so perfect as to add brilliance rather than creating a dimming flaw. Go in safety.

First sitting with L., October 3, 1961. L. &. H. This is the *complete* transcript:

Q. Who is here? **A.** Ryoll.

The disk moved immediately, without further questions, into the following:

Let the burdens of the day slip further into the dream state from which they came.

Q. Who are you? **A.** I am little known but even so small a part of God's creation can light the way if the grace of God is glowing in his heart. I am in L.'s sphere of guardianship.

Excerpt, October 27, 1961, L. & H. Again a message from "Ryoll":

Each child of Christ is held dear to our Father, not because his fellow man calls him a Christian but because he possesses a little more understanding of the mutuality of both love and responsibility between him and his Creator. Those who have the consciousness of the Christ spirit within may walk ever in the light of our Father's love. It is so by His Word.

Excerpt, November 3, 1961, L. & H. During this sitting we were feeling very gay and laughed a great deal. "Ryoll" again was the name given, as was true of every sitting I had with L.

Q. Where do you live? **A.** Know that we all live in the Kingdom of God which has no limits or boundaries.

Q. Are you annoyed with us because we are laughing so much? **A.** Laughter is one of the sounds too seldom heard in your world. Never fear censure for expressing joy. Such sounds are as the music of the spheres. Laughter is one of man's ways of expressing faith as true laughter cannot come from a heart which is fearful. Be strong in faith to be rich in joy. As all loving fathers should, our Father rejoices to see His children trusting and happy.

Excerpt, January 2, 1962, L. & H. Disk started moving as soon as we touched it:

Ryoll is here. Righteousness is admirable only when it is self-contained. To inflict that characteristic commonly called righteousness makes it righteouslessness. It is a quality which grows in beauty only when it is discovered by others' awareness of it as opposed to self-projection.

Q. Does this message apply to us? **A.** To lots of people this is a very common frailty. Each man demonstrates the true level of his spirituality in humility.

Excerpt, January 25, 1962, L. & H.

Q. Who is here? **A.** Pause for a moment.

We sat for a few moments with our fingers resting on the planchette which finally started. It started immediately to give a message:
Sometimes circumstances create a void in the vibratory stream which causes unnecessary dissipation of energy from both sides. Ryoll is here.

Q. Did we do something wrong? **A.** It is the fault of a personal nature. Tonight the psychic stream is disrupted by a turbulence outside your sphere.
Q. Has it cleared? **A.** All is well.
Q. Will the coming configuration of planets affect us in any way? **A.** It is to be expected that such conflict will leave its mark on many. The degree of influence varies vitally with the rate of vibration each has attained in his own evolvement. You individually will experience only that which you accept as your own. The choice is yours.

Closing message:
Fill your heart with love, your soul with light and your mind with charity for fulfillment of God's plan.

Excerpt, April 5, 1962, L. & H. This message from "Ryoll" is my favorite of them all:

Heartbreak is the great teacher even for the highly evolved on your plane. It is with falling tears that the stumbling block of pride is most frequently swept from the path to spiritual perfection. Grief is not punishment but a tempering process. No grief can obscure the glory of the love and compassion in the overall plan God has for each of us in His creation. In those times of trial hold fast; God's strength is your strength. Comfort is within even as He is. Mortal mind cannot perceive the value of suffering until it is no longer necessary.

Excerpt, no date, L. & H. A message which came with no questions asked:

Ryoll is here. Each dawn brings to those who are willing to see, evidence of fatherly love in its most perfect expression. Only a loving father nightly extends to constantly wayward children many times undeserved forgiveness with opportunities to begin anew all things without reproach. Each dawn is symbolic of our Father's generous offer of eternal supply of all good. As dawns are unlimited so is God's compassion and love. In the growing light of each dawn open your heart to the greatest light of all—the light which guides, lifts and heals is yours verily by grace.

Excerpt, another undated one, L. & H.:

Spend a right proportion of your allotted time time (sic) developing spiritual gifts, for the time spent in cultivating spiritual gifts is rewarding in more ways than mortal mind can properly evaluate. Seek your gifts and use them.

Excerpt, undated, sitters A. & H. There was no name given:

Ignorance of nature's laws brings distress even as ignorance of civil laws results in trouble. Elimination of ignorance brings the greatest hope of serenity, which is the sweetest fruit of the seeds of understanding.

Excerpt, February 22, 1962, A. & H. No name given:

Every day is a new opportunity to grow in all manner. Man must realize that what he harvests is determined by the quality of faith, abundance of love and mercy plowed into the furrows which are each hour of his earthly span.

Undated message from "Ryoll," L. & H. sitting:

Open all natural channels to receive new strength and power. Leisure time is often valuable for browsing through your collection of experiences. Relish the sweet and discard the less noble. As you window-shop your soul be sure that each experience is worth the price paid. Use some of each hour of leisure to add to all good by acknowledging that which is yours already. All is ready to be claimed by you. Choose wisely.

PERSONAL AND PRECOGNITIVE MESSAGES

Although I have never received messages of a personal, precognitive nature, I know of several people who have. These are perfectly sane, rational people and the material received has been evidential of knowledge beyond that in their consciousness.

One woman I know received exact directions to the location of some money which had disappeared. It was not her money, she had not lost it, but she was in the house where it had been last seen. Her faithful Ouija board gave the information which led to the recovery of the money.

Another woman received the precise directions to locate a stone which had flown out of her nephew's hand while he was polishing it on his grinding wheel. Hours of search failed to reveal where the stone had landed. He telephoned his aunt and asked her to ask her Ouija board where it was. She sat down alone with her board, asked the question, received an answer and then called her nephew to relay the directions. He looked and found the stone lodged on top of a window frame in his workroom.

This same woman received details of an accident in which one of her family had been involved. She knew nothing about the accident at the time she was sitting with her board. Her family was on a vacation trip. When she next heard from them they told her about the accident and the injuries sustained. Although this woman worked the board alone, as a rule, she had witnesses to the receipt of these messages. They are right on all counts to the extent that she no longer questions the information she receives.

Another woman of my acquaintance had guests one afternoon and the Ouija board was in play during the course of part of the conversation. After one of the guests left for home, the rest of the women continued to use the board. Within a short time, the telephone rang; it was the woman who had gone home early. She was in a panic—her little girl was missing and had been the object of search by neighbors and other family members for several hours. The hostess, an old hand with the Ouija board, asked immediately that the board give her information about the whereabouts of the little girl. Without any hesitancy at all the board spelled out the information that the child had crawled under one of the beds and had fallen asleep. She passed the word to the mother who ran to check the story. She found the child sound asleep under the bed!

One of my fellow researchers has told me of a family which uses the Ouija board with astounding success. I do not know the family personally, although I know of them, since one of the daughters is a prize winning writer. The mother and two of the daughters in this instance do receive definite and accurate results in the area of predictions. According to the reports I have received, they are apprised of events of a national and world-wide nature, as well as those which apply only to their own circle of family and friends.

In the interest of conserving book space I have not included here messages from my own collection which are not strictly of a philosophical nature. There is almost enough material in these records to make a book in itself.

A CASE OF SPIRIT DEVELOPMENT

"F" and I had many enjoyable evenings with our "friends," one of our favorite contacts being the one which called himself "Lolly." Here was a contact with a delightful sense of humor. Our first experience with this entity was very strange. Purportedly it was made before he realized he was "dead." As time passed the humor changed from a rather sarcastic and frightened sort of humor to a marvelous kind of wit, tempered with gentleness and understanding.

Whatever the motivating force which moved the planchette, it certainly had intelligence. It was almost like seeing a person in a strange and bewildering environment making an adjustment of tremendous proportions. We thoroughly enjoyed this story as it unfolded week after week. We lost contact with this entity when he was supposedly advanced to a place where his responsibility was such that there was no time for further contact.

THE BOARD AS A STEP IN PSYCHIC DEVELOPMENT

The fact that I no longer use a Ouija board does not mean that I feel that it is a "low" form of contact. One does advance in all areas of endeavor and becomes involved with matters which are time consuming. It is necessary to make a choice when time becomes limited. I do recommend that anyone who has the desire to experiment with the board do so. It is no lower in the scale of psychic experimentation than any other method suitable for beginners. It may be that it is simple—but that is no drawback, unless one is more interested in making an impression than he is in attaining results.

As for where the information comes from—who can say? I'd be most happy to know that I had the wisdom and beauty in my consciousness that we have drawn from the board. If it's from my own subconscious all I can say is that it's a very inexpensive method of psychoanalysis!

SUMMARY OF CHAPTER TEN

1. Many people claim Ouija boards are dangerous, but the danger is in the consciousness of the operator, not the board itself.
2. Sometimes peculiar physical reactions accompany change of "controls."
3. Rules may be entirely different for success at Ouija boards with change of operators since the widely variable human attitude is the most vital factor in its operation.
4. Results seem to be more philosophical and evidential if questions are kept at a minimum.
5. Ouija boards have been used with success for precognitive messages on personal, national and world matters.
6. Much information, not in the normal range of knowledge of the operators, has been obtained from Ouija boards—this includes finding lost objects, events taking place at the time of the sitting, and items concerning strangers.

ELEVEN

Differences Between

Possession and

Obsession

Possession is that state which results from a discarnate entity entering the body and controlling the consciousness of a living being.

Obsession is that state of existence where there is no actual entry by such a discarnate entity, but external control is exercised.

Possession is an intrusion; obsession is an influence.

Since time immemorial there have been two schools of thought on the reality of obsession and possession—one of total acceptance of the possibility, and one of total rejection. For thousands of years, those who believe in the possibility of such control have used amulets, good luck pieces, and charms to ward off the evil influence, or have used rites of exorcism for its expulsion if it is already manifest in a person. This chapter will deal with the elements of handling these two states or conditions.

Much has been written about these two conditions. It is one of the largest single-entry subjects in *An Encyclopaedia of Occultism* by Lewis Spence. There is scarcely a book of religious philosophy, including the Holy Bible, that does not contain episodes which describe obsession and possession. Every periodical available to the student of the occult or paranormal carries accounts of such occurrences, which appear to take place with as much frequency today as in the so-called "dark ages."

SIMILARITIES OF POSSESSION AND OBSESSION

There is much similarity between the two conditions, since both are marked by personality changes usually attributed to mental illness or moral disintegration. Some of the old beliefs associated such conditions with evil spirits or demons, while others associated them with the gods. If the personality affected showed more virtue or functioned more productively after the control began to manifest, no doubt all connected with the victim would thank their lucky stars for the improvement. Because of this they would not consult with priests or sorcerers to exorcise the invader, which no doubt is the reason there are more records of evil invaders than good ones.

Although many hold to the idea that good spirits would not be guilty of such a thing as trespass, I can't say that I concur with this. I can understand that highly evolved consciousness would make it necessary that the cause or ultimate end be a good one before such an action would be carried out, but I can think of many reasons for good spirits to have need of a body in which to express, and they might very well avail themselves of the opportunity to take over a body which might be slated for evacuation. It seems reasonable to me that it might be more expedient for an evolved soul to be assigned to a matured body than for him to have to start from babyhood and grow to the age where he could accomplish his mission.

I can understand the reluctance to believe that good spirits would choose to take over another's body, but it seems to me that this is only improbable if the body occupant is forcibly ejected before his "lease" is up. Nature wastes nothing and it isn't feasible, in my opinion, that a perfectly healthy body should be permitted to return to dust because its tenant had to move out, any more than such should be done with a house because the owner moved out.

Man's wrong concepts

Our doctrines on the nature of death, in the sense of orthodox religious teachings, are entirely too morbid. Death is as beautiful as birth; the process of dying is not free from its distressing aspect most times, but neither is the birth process. Man has made them so.

Everything we can comprehend is comparative by opposites; why not possession? We can grant that influence can be good, so why can we not have good obsessions, also? I firmly believe that we do have more reports of the less desirable possessions and obsessions, but I also believe that the margin of good is at least as great as the margin of the unfortunate. We just don't hear of them.

Not all cases of obsession or possession are continuous. Some have a suggestion of alternate invasion and absence on the part of the second personality. This is probably most commonly manifested in cases of kleptomania, alcoholism, and similar cases of recurring bad habits in otherwise normal people. The danger in this line of thought is that it supplies an excuse for weakness, although I can see that it might be applicable with justification in some instances.

The spiritualistic concept

In the spiritualistic concept, the world is peopled with earthbound discarnates who are held here by physical or material desires which cannot be satisfied without the use of a physical body. In order to appease these appetites or desires, the restless spirit searches until he finds a vulnerable person, one who shows an inclination to participate in whatever activity is necessary to satisfy his craving. At a propitious moment (for him), he pushes the consciousness of the rightful owner out of the body, and takes over himself for his own purposes.

As soon as the thirst, appetite, lust or whatever, is sated, he leaves the body for re-entry by the rightful occupant. If the case is one of obsession, the need is such that a vicarious pleasure is enough, so the controlling entity merely ceases to impress the consciousness of his victim as soon as he is gratified. Once satisfactory results are obtained through an individual, that person is at the mercy of the discarnate until he learns what happened and what he must do to protect himself from future control by invasion of his body or his mind.

Mind and body invaders and pirates

Clairvoyants say that there are mind and body pirates which can be seen as they lurk around all places where these potential vehicles can be found. For example, the spirit of a deceased dope addict will be more likely to find a body he can "use" if he frequents a spot where narcotics are used—in massive doses for legitimate reasons or at a party where novices seek thrills. Spirits who had been alcoholics at the time of their death are apt to find a satisfactory instrument around a bar or drinking party. Compulsive gambling habits may cause a spirit to seek a vicarious pleasure through weak-willed people given to immoderate gambling since he can influence them to wager beyond all reasonable limits.

Visible characteristics

It is claimed by psychics who can see them that these earthbound spirits are recognizable because of an ugly coloration in their forms. The same colors, but to a slighter degree, are visible in the auras (see chapter on auras) of their victims—hence the means of identification of the type of person the discarnate can expect to satisfy his particular need. In cases where the vicarious pleasure derived through obsession is not enough, many clairvoyants say they can see the actual possession of the body take place.

CASES OF ALCOHOLIC POSSESSION

A nurse who frequently attended alcoholic patients told me that she often saw the possessing discarnate entity around one of the patients with whom I was acquainted. She said that she had described the invader to members of the patient's family. They told her that the description exactly matched a very close relative who had been deceased a few years—a man who had been a most unfortunate influence on the patient during his lifetime. As is often true in cases of possession, the patient in this case assumed an entirely different personality immediately before starting on a drinking bout and did not resume her own personality until she regained consciousness after many hours of terrible suffering.

I have had a measure of success in assisting alcoholics rehabilitate themselves. Many times I have seen what could be cases of possession manifest. Since I am not clairvoyant to an exceptional degree, I have never *seen* an invader, but I can well know that they are there by their psychic presence which I can sense.

Although there is much support for the belief in the possession-obsession theory, I do not believe that in every case in which an offender says, "I could not help myself; I don't know why I did it," is the presence of a spirit a valid excuse. I must admit, however, that circumstances in many instances would indicate that this defense has merit. Some theologians are obviously in accord with this belief, since some orthodox churches still employ exorcising rites.

Some years ago, in the convent of the Franciscan Sisters at Earling, Iowa, the reported rites of exorcism were performed by the Reverend Theophilus Riesinger. This case is recorded in an official pamphlet of the orthodox church. *Fate Magazine,* in the summer of 1958, carried a series of articles which gave many gruesome details of this case. It is recommended reading only for those with strong constitutions.

As I read accounts of this sort I must remind myself that these occurrences are taking place during my lifetime—not back in the Middle Ages.

MISCELLANEOUS CASES OF REPORTED POSSESSION

Some classic accounts of possession which occurred in the 19th century are recounted in modern terms by well-known researchers in the area of parapsychology and psychism. In *Tomorrow Magazine* there was an interesting article entitled "Alabama's Sleeping Preacher," by Edmond Gibson, formerly connected with the Parapsychology Department at Duke University. Frank Edward's fascinating book, *Strange People,* contains a detailed article entitled "The Incredible Case of Lurancy Vennum." Mr. Edward's book also contains a modern case of possession in "The Possession of Maria Talarico," a strange but documented case which took place in Italy in 1936.

A little possessed

Following is a local case which had all the earmarks of possession of a little boy by his deceased grandfather. The child, about three and a half years old at the time of his grandfather's death, had been unusually close to his grandparents—he and his grandfather had been inseparable. Although his grandfather had had several severe heart attacks before the fatal one, the child told his grandfather goodby with an air of finality at the onset of the fatal attack.

After the death of the man, the child soon began to show many of the characteristics and mannerisms of the deceased. He even began to participate in matters which had been of moment to the man during his lifetime—matters which had been of no interest to the child during his grandfather's lifetime. It was so noticeable that friends began to remark that the child no longer acted like a little boy but a man. Alarmed by the strange behavior of the child, the family consulted their priest and exorcism was employed. The child returned to normal and after that lived according to his age.

SUCCESSIVE SPIRIT POSSESSIONS

Another local case bears out the theory held by some that during critical illness, sometimes the soul leaves the body, but death does not appear to take place because another soul takes possession and reanimates the newly deserted body. Serious illness frequently does cause some personality change, but this particular incident included such a radical change that one is almost forced to conclude that two separate entities were occupants of one body—not concurrently but successively.

Because the principal involved in this case was a member of a large organization for women, there were many witnesses to the apparent substitution of spirit. I have the highest esteem for my source of information, and I am sure that there are many other witnesses to vouch for the truth of the story.

My informant was a good friend and neighbor of about eight years' standing, when her husband's work took them away from this city for about two and a half years. When they finally were able to move back here again, she took up most of the activities she had had with various groups to which she previously had belonged.

A church group luncheon was one of the first functions she attended, where she had many old friends she had looked forward to seeing again. She had been a member of this group for about ten years.

During the luncheon one of the women at her table puzzled her; the woman obviously knew her, called her by her first name, asked her about her family members by name and knew about her changes of residence. But she could not place this woman to save her life!

At the first opportune moment she asked another guest who the woman was. She immediately recognized the name when she was told, but could not connect it in any way with the woman in question. The name she was given was that of a woman she had known before she went away—but things just didn't fit.

The woman she had known had been a petite, immaculately groomed young woman; this woman was almost grossly fat, slovenly and apparently middle-aged. At the earliest convenient time she made it a point to try to straighten out this muddle.

About a year and a half before the luncheon, she was told, the young woman had been hospitalized by a serious illness. All hope for her recovery had been abandoned when she slipped into a deep coma. Then a seeming miracle happened—new life flowed in and the patient recovered.

After she returned home from the hospital, however, it was discovered that her whole personality had changed. Instead of the devoted wife and mother who had gone to the hospital, the family found themselves with a wife and mother who was totally indifferent and actually callous toward her small children. As she convalesced, her personality change became more accentuated. Is possession too unreasonable a theory to apply here? What other explanation fits as well?

Thirty Years Among the Dead is an account of the years of research into obsession and possession conducted by Dr. and Mrs. Carl A. Wickland. Dr. Wickland, an M.D., wrote this record of his 30 years of experimental research in normal and paranormal psychology.

Mrs. Wickland was a medium to whom Dr. Wickland would transfer possessing spirits from the bodies of patients he believed to be victims of such intrusion. He would then question the entities while they were in possession of his wife's body instead of the supposed mental patient from whose body he had persuaded them.

This book, written about twenty years before Dr. Wickland's death in 1945, was out of print for some years, but it is once again being published. It is considered a valid study in abnormal psychology and in many ways far in advance of present day psychiatry.

DEMONOLOGY (DEMON POSSESSION)

Professor William James wrote, in the "Proceedings of the Society for Psychical Research," that in his opinion the theory of demon possession would come into its own because only blind ignorance on the part of conventional science could exclude it much longer. This is a powerful statement, and I would not argue with anyone of the stature of William James—when there is so much evidence that he is right.

Some of the researchers in the investigation of possession-obsession have concluded that shock treatments and hydrotherapy sessions in the treatment of mental illness are effective because they render the physical body so uncomfortable that the invading spirit deserts the body he has stolen. The rightful inhabitant may then return. This is plausible since an interloper would be less reluctant to abandon a place of residence than would a rightful owner. This would particularly be true if the trespasser knew that he could move in somewhere else. It would not be long before a dislodged spirit could find another body into which he could move without too much trouble.

Some time ago I heard an experience recounted by a young man who practiced astral projection. He claimed that upon one occasion when he returned from astral flight he found his body had been taken over by an undesirable entity. He said that he had a terrifying battle with this spirit in order to gain re-entry. I was quite surprised to hear that he had such a harrowing time, since he was supposedly well versed in psychic protection. However, I had no reason to doubt the truth of his account as he had nothing to gain from an admission that he had slipped up on protecting himself from such an eventuality.

HOW TO PROTECT YOURSELF AGAINST ADVERSE POSSESSION

One of the most effective protections against such an experience, whether during an astral projection or otherwise, is the development of a *strong aura*. The methods for doing this are given in the chapter on auras. Invasion is possible only when the consciousness is lowered by negative mental, physical or emotional conditions. A high rate of vibration so strengthens and brightens the aura, which is visible to the discarnates, that they don't bother to make the effort to intrude. It doesn't hurt to take that ounce of prevention—it's too late to shop for hospitalization insurance when one is on the operating table!

SUMMARY OF CHAPTER ELEVEN

1. Possession is an influence from inside; obsession is an influence from an external source.
2. Both possession and obsession result in personality changes, occasional or constant, better or worse.
3. Clairvoyants claim to see discarnate invaders hovering about, waiting to invade bodies or control minds of vulnerable victims.
4. Recognized cases of possession or obsession are frequently treated successfully with exorcism.
5. It is believed that during critical illness or death, the body may be "taken" or even reanimated by a discarnate, thus explaining personality changes which sometimes follow such conditions as recovery from near fatal illness or apparent death.
6. Exorcism or shock treatment may effect a cure, but a strong aura provides protection against invasion or control.

TWELVE

How to Develop

Your Psychometry Powers

P sychometry can be defined as "1. The science of the measurement of psychophysical processes, especially of their accuracy or duration in time; mental testing. 2. Divination by physical contact or proximity of the properties of things touched or approached." Our consideration in this chapter is primarily with the second definition.

WOMEN MORE SUCCESSFUL IN PSYCHOMETRY

The "reading" of objects by handling them is a phase of psychic ability latent in one of ten men and one of four women to a remarkable degree, according to some researchers who have determined this ratio as a result of carefully conducted tests. I know enough people who developed this ability with such amazing ease that I agree that it is certainly one of the most commonly found and easily developed psychic gifts.

The fact that it seems more prevalent in women than men may be because women are more prone to take such things seriously and as a result are more patient in working for the unfoldment of this latent faculty. Certainly men do have this phase of ESP to a great degree, as most of the world's best known psychometrists are men.

Peter Hurkos, perhaps the world's most publicized psychometrist a few years ago, did not cultivate his ability, if one can believe the story of his life. He acquired it from a severe head injury. This would seem to indicate that there is a part of the physical brain which merely needs stimulation or opening to activate psychic ability. I am not certain enough of this to recommend that we try beating each other over the head in an attempt to step up psychic ability, however.

PSYCHOMETRY ART EASILY ACQUIRED

I do not mean to imply that *anyone* can become a truly great psychometrist with the remarkable degree of accuracy and efficiency that has been attained by those we read about in newspapers and books. But I sincerely believe that thousands of people could develop this gift if they would only try.

Before one tries psychometry it is well to understand a little about it.

Basis of psychometry

Every object has its own magnetic field or aura. In this field are vibrations which tell the story of the object's history, relative to its owners' (past and present) environment and its own. A good psychometrist, as he holds an object, picks up these vibrations and describes the impressions he receives. Some psychometrists work in the trance state, or semi-trance state, but many work in a normal state of consciousness.

The greatest difficulty seems to be the development of the ability to give voice to impressions as they come, without alteration because of rationalization or coloration. One must learn to "listen" and "feel" and then express freely what he picks up, regardless of how ridiculous or improbable the statements may seem to him.

A first attempt to psychometrize

My own first attempt at psychometry was typical of many persons' first attempt, I am sure.

A friend and I had spent the night at a mutual friend's home because of a violent thunder storm which made it impossible to get back to our own hometown. Since we did not often get to see one another we decided to spend the night in conversation rather than sleep. As is usual in my circle of acquaintances, the discussion was about ESP and the occult.

When we touched upon the subject of psychometry our hostess arose, went into another room and came back with a lovely piece of embroidered ribbon in her hand.

She handed it to me, saying as she did so, "See what you can get from this."

A strange feeling of revulsion came over me and it was with much reluctance that I kept the ribbon in my hand.

Almost without volition I blurted out "New Orleans."

I was not only surprised, I felt a little foolish because I was well aware of the fact that my hostess had recently received a box of her possessions from that town.

However, right on the heels of this came a picture (a mental one, of course) of people in formal evening attire. They were milling about in a magnificent house-like public place in great excitement. In another moment I saw a burst of flames. After that nothing.

I put the ribbon down with a feeling of great relief.

My hostess said the ribbon had been given to her when she was a little girl. It was a portion of a much larger piece which her father had kept as a souvenir of an experience he had had as a young man.

He was a guest one night in an exclusive gambling club in one of New Orleans' old mansions. A professional man whose position demanded circumspect behavior had the misfortune to be in love with one of the "house girls" of whom he was extremely jealous. She was not as faithful to him as he wished her to be. On this particular night he became so enraged that he tried to kill her. In the ensuing confusion and excitement, someone accidentally set the place on fire. Her father tugged on a ribbon bell-pull to summon help and it broke off as he yanked on it. In his agitation he rammed the ribbon in his pocket without thinking and discovered it when he got home. Many years later he told his daughter the story and gave her a piece of the portion he had kept as a memento of the exciting night.

One evening two school teachers interested in parapsychology came to my home for some conversation about ESP. Neither of them was familiar with psychometry, but after I had explained it to them and recounted the above experience they wanted me to try it for them.

One of the women took an object from her purse and handed it to me. I did not look at it; I simply closed my hand over it as she placed it on my palm. Instantly, even though I was talking to the other woman at the time, I had a vivid impression of very short reddish hair, a definitely mannish haircut. Then I could almost see, in silhouette, a stocky figure. Somehow I sensed that this object had been a gift from this man and that there was a feeling of dissatisfaction or unhappiness in this relationship—on whose part I did not know. Finally, I "saw" the color gray and felt that this was in some way important in this man's life, either car, home, uniform or some other major part. Then came the blankness again.

Sparse as the details were, I was surprised and gratified when they were verified with the exception of the gray, which could not be placed. The object, incidentally, was a pair of earrings which had been a gift to the lady from the gentleman described.

A friend handed me a pen which she asked me to psychometrize. She remarked as she gave it to me that I did not know the person to whom it belonged. As I took it I felt an impact on the back of my head, just above my left ear, followed by a feeling of growing pressure in my body. I could only explain this as the feeling of high blood pressure, although I really don't *know* how this feels. Sometimes it is more difficult to describe an impression than it is to feel it in the first place.

The impressions which followed were less physical in nature. I knew, for example, that the owner lived so far away that he had contact with my friend and her family only about every six months (except by correspondence). The next impression was one of a tall, lean, gray-haired man. Then I saw a great many boats of all types, but none of them seemed to be moving, a detail which I could not understand.

Since I did not receive any detailed or colorful impressions, the statements I have put down here are almost precisely as I gave them aloud as they came.

I was delighted when my friend told me that the pen belonged to her brother-in-law. His work was with boats while they were in a large port, and his home was about 600 miles away so they saw him only on vacations (his in the winter and her husband's in the summer). She could not identify the lean, gray-haired man, nor could she be sure of the physical condition I had described, although the most recent letter received from her sister-in-law had mentioned that her husband had not been feeling well and was going to a doctor for diagnosis. We generously, among ourselves, concluded that the gray-haired man had given the pen to the brother-in-law as a gift.

My only purpose in taking so much time and space relating my own experiences is to make clear the simple way the impressions come to a beginner in psychometry. They seem to be simple and unrelated thoughts, yet when these foolish-seeming thoughts are voiced exactly as they come, they often turn out to be highly significant.

I am sure that everyone in the beginning feels a reluctance to say what comes into his mind while experimenting in this way, but it is an absolute *must*. No thought should be disregarded as irrelevant—present it and let the other person determine its value.

How psychometric impressions come

To illustrate further how impressions come, I will describe two experiences of my own.

One afternoon I was at the home of the school teacher previously mentioned, and she asked me to do a couple of readings of objects in order that her young daughter might see how it worked. She handed me something which I could tell was an article of jewelry because of the feel of it. *I did not look at it* because I didn't want to color my impressions by knowing whether it belonged to the mother or the daughter.

My first impression was wrong—I thought that it was a gift from a member of the family, but I was right that it had been a gift from a man. Next, I had the feeling that this man was unusually meticulous about his person and was well-dressed as a matter of personal pride. I had the impression that the man was a husky, almost rugged type, but I did not know whether he was the same man I had described in my previous reading for this particular woman.

The last impression to come was that this had been a gift of unusual significance, a special occasion surprise as opposed to a birthday or Christmas present. I felt that it was something which had been seen or admired by the recipient, and the man had bought it just as a nice surprise. I still did not know to whom the article belonged.

I did not question for details after I finished because I did not wish to pry, but both the mother and daughter said that I had been accurate except for the statement that the man was a member of their family.

The mother then went out of the room and came back with a small package in her hand. She said that she had purposely wrapped this article since she felt that if I saw it I might begin to rationalize. It was a package somewhat in shape and size similar to the kind of box one gets with costume jewelry sets. The paper in which it was loosely wrapped was the printed type of gift paper—not the special occasion kind, but the pastel floral type.

Instantly when I touched the package I felt a foreign influence. I remarked that I felt that it concerned someone or something away from the North American continent. I also had an immediate impression of a woman with gray hair, whom I described as being in her late sixties and with an accent of someone from Central Europe.

The mother shook her head in bewilderment and said she could see no connection.

A feeling of being very warm and tired, particularly in my legs, made me express the opinion that this was something which had been shopped for on a hot day and had been found only after much shopping around in numerous stores.

Again the mother shook her head. She could see absolutely no connection, she said.

The daughter, however, was bursting with excitement. She reminded her mother that the paper in which the object was wrapped was the very same wrapper which covered the gift she had given her mother for Mother's Day a few weeks earlier.

She then said that she had shopped for some time, walking from one shop to another, tired and hot, before she found what she wanted. Then the saleswoman from whom she made the purchase was an elderly woman with a German accent!

PSYCHOMETRIZING WITH ESP

There is another form of psychometrizing which is very popular with groups like the ones which gathered at my home to experiment (in a non-scientific way) with the various types of ESP. It is very difficult to evaluate the results on a percentage-of-hits basis, since the range of possibility is indeterminate—the choice of subject matter is unlimited.

Each person in the group draws on a small piece of paper, without regard to artistic ability, a picture of an object of his own choosing. As he draws he thinks of the object and its sensory attributes—color, odor, weight, texture, temperature, anything which stimulates the senses when one has the real object available to him. He then folds the paper and puts a three digit number on the outside of the folded piece—this is to identify it as his drawing. No one is to know the particular number of any paper except his own. All papers are then placed in a bowl or on a tray. Each person then draws in turn from the collection a paper other than his own.

As soon as everyone has one of the folded papers in his hand, he immediately takes note of any thoughts which come into his mind. We usually sit quietly for a minute or two—it is best not to sit *too* long before giving the impressions aloud or writing them down, as rationalizing makes one tend to discount the first thoughts, and these are most likely to be the correct ones. When the conscious mind begins to take over it closes out subconscious reactions, and it is the subconscious which gives the best answers in these tests.

PSYCHOMETRIC ACCURACIES CAN VARY

Since even the best psychometrists in the world cannot demonstrate 100 percent accuracy, do not be discouraged by failures. There are times when I amaze myself with *exact details,* then again there are times when I draw a complete blank or get impressions that are so wrong they are almost humorous. In one session I have been able to get five out of six articles—not to name the object, but to get so many of its attributes as to exclude chance or guess as possibilities.

In order to illustrate what may be considered a high degree of accuracy without actually naming the object drawn, I give the following examples:

The impression received and given aloud was a feeling of forward motion, a bell-shaped object compared to an auto horn in shape but not sound; the sound was described as being more like a "marine" horn. The object drawn was a clarinet, drawn by the mother of a boy who was on his way to march in a football parade in a town about 65 miles away; he was one of the bandsmen.

The impression was given as a "sensation" across the eyebrows and "looking through something." The object drawn was a pair of eyeglasses.

This impression seemed impossibly confused, but it proved to be interestingly accurate in the end. It seemed that the object was liquid and solid, at the same time; also there was a strong impression of fragrance. The feeling of confusion was dispelled when the drawing turned out to be a bottle of perfume.

When one considers the many thousands of articles which might be depicted inside the folded papers, it is easy to see that the pertinent details such as the ones described above are far beyond chance.

There have been many times, in group experiments such as these, when the same reactions are picked up by several participants—even when the objects on the papers they have drawn have no similarity to the impressions they have received. It would appear in these instances that thought transference is a stronger aptitude in the principals involved than is psychometry.

Since we never attempted these experiments unless all of the persons involved were sincerely interested and would not mislead or improvise in order to "show off," we felt that each one contributed only honest reactions. It is very important in this work that one's fellow experimenters be completely trustworthy. The life-of-the-party type or the "show-off" who is never wrong lend nothing to this type of activity.

HOW TO DEVELOP SENSITIVITY

To develop sensitivity in the hands for psychometric demonstration, one may practice by slowly lowering the hands at the fingertips into water (of body temperature) in a bowl, which should be out of the line of vision. Without visual perception, it is difficult to tell when the fingers touch and enter the water. With practice the sensitivity is increased.

Another simple exercise to heighten reaction is to put various materials of similar texture and weight, such as salt, sugar, and sand, to mention just three of many, into identical envelopes, and try to feel the difference simply by holding them in the hands one at a time.

Most psychometrists "read" by holding the article in one or both hands; others place the object against the forehead or the solar plexus, the region commonly referred to as the "pit of the stomach," but which is approximately at the point just below the breast where the ribs feel as if they begin to separate. Try all of the positions, as results may prove to be much more successful for you in one of the less commonly used positions.

One of the aspects peculiar to psychometry is that some people are sensitive only to metal objects, while others may be sensitive only to cloth, paper, minerals or some other specific material. Do not give up trying to "read" objects until you try all types of materials.

Distance between the psychic and the owner of the object being "read" does not seem to matter to most psychometrists; proximity of the article is all that matters.

Lost persons have been found by psychometrists who have handled some article owned by the missing person, whether the missing person is living or dead. There are numerous accounts of this accomplishment on record, as well as the solution of crimes through this means of looking into the field of action around objects.

PSYCHOMETRY IN SOLVING CRIMES

As an aside here, I might say that in Europe and in the British Isles it is not uncommon for police to consult a psychometrist in the work of solving crimes. It is comparatively infrequent in the United States, since we seem to be many years behind in the recognition of ESP as a valid practice. There is no stigma of any kind attached to the psychic in other countries, unless it is that with which the individual brands himself because of malpractice.

VARIOUS USES OF PSYCHOMETRY

I have had well-developed psychometrists "read" for me on only two occasions. Both read my past with startling accuracy and made some prognostications about my future with what I hope is equal accuracy.

The most detailed reading was made from a ring which I had worn for years. The briefer reading came from a bracelet which I had owned for some time but had only worn twice. I do not know whether the bracelet did not possess enough of my vibrations or the reader was not in good form, but I rather suspect the former was the case since the few details given were absolutely true.

It is my belief that psychometry attempts will bring the most surprising results of any of the psychic experiments a layman might undertake. Many of the "esoteric schools" and "secret brotherhoods" start their teachings with simple psychometric experiments; no doubt they are well aware of the high degree of accuracy obtainable by novices and are also aware that nothing impresses a beginner like success in the very opening lesson-experiments.

It is usually suggested that the student attempt to psychometrize letters before opening them. This is good practice and anyone who will hold a letter in his hand and keep his mind open to receive impressions will no doubt be astounded by his ability to determine something pertinent about its contents.

Practiced psychometrists can hold a very old object—an article of great antiquity—and have fascinating stories unfold in his mind. Most of these are next to impossible to verify, but they are interesting, nonetheless.

Perhaps, despite all that has been said here about the ease with which psychometry can be done by even the beginner, you might feel as a young woman did who came to my home. Our conversation eventually reached the subject of psychometry. I told her of my own experience, explained some of the theories about what makes it work, and finally persuaded her to hold a ring of mine to see what she could do with it.

Very skeptically she took the ring in her hand. Instantly she had an impression of a man, properly placed him in his relationship to me, then proceeded to belittle the impression on the grounds that this was the result of pure reason or rationalization.

Her words of rejection were scarcely out of her mouth when she looked rather bewildered and began describing a scene in considerable detail. She described a room, some of the furnishings, and gave a character sketch of a child. Her remarks were interspersed with such comments as "This doesn't make any sense," "I don't know why I should think of this," and similar observations. Her bewilderment at the vividness of the thoughts made it impossible to question the reality of them. Her bewilderment turned to almost open-mouthed astonishment when I told her she had exactly described circumstances at the time the ring was purchased. As simply as that she proved to herself that she, too, could do psychometry.

A particular warning

In fairness to yourself when you start doing tests, be sure that the object you are working with is one which is handled by the person you are reading for almost exclusively. Eyeglasses, cigarette lighters, rings, etc. are good because these are things which are rarely used by anyone but the owner, who usually has them on his person most of the time. Such things as money, car keys, and so on which might in the course of their use pass through many hands are not good objects to work with—they absorb too much of other people and the details cannot be verified in many instances.

I feel strongly that the layman can do much to help us advance in many ways by practicing this simple and almost universal gift of psychometry. As yet, we have only scratched the surface of this promising aid to a more serene life of enjoyment through daily use of psychometry.

SUMMARY OF CHAPTER TWELVE

1. Psychometry, the ability to "read" objects, is the most easily developed psychic ability, being readily available to one of ten men and one of four women.

2. Every object (except those made of lead) radiates its own aura which always carries the story of its owner and/or environment.

3. In practicing psychometry you must develop the habit of giving all impressions without rationalization or alteration, and no thought should be disregarded as irrelevant.

4. There are several simple but evidential experiments included in this chapter for you to test your ability to psychometrize.

5. Since sensitivity may be greater to one material than another, try objects of paper, wood, metal, fabric, etc. in your tests.

6. Psychometry, highly developed, is used by police departments in crime work all over the world.

THIRTEEN

Psychic Photography:

Its Techniques

and Applications

In 1862 in Boston, Massachusetts, a photographer named Mumler produced what was purported to be a spirit photograph. In the intervening years there have been many thousands of such photographs produced, some obvious frauds and others apparently genuine pictures of spirit forms. This chapter deals with various methods of exposing photographic film for psychic demonstration.

WHAT FILM CAN RECORD THAT HUMAN EYE CANNOT SEE

Photographic film is sensitive to rays that the human eye cannot see, evidently, since there have been many spirit photographs examined and proven to be unretouched after exposure. These show forms which were not visible to witnesses to the experiments.

Spirit photography has been achieved under test conditions, the use of various lighting conditions from total darkness to complete visibility, special film in ordinary holders or ordinary film in special holders, ordinary film in ordinary cameras, on film without use of a camera, on photographic paper without use of film, in seance sittings with mediums, and spontaneously without the presence of a medium.

In this field there is an abundance of material that is supposed to be spirit photographs which are really quite ordinary pictures, the shadows of which are so placed as to suggest hidden faces and forms to anyone of imagination. These are not examples of psychic photography although they are often printed in publications under the title of psychic photography.

Closely allied to spirit photography is a phenomenon known as thought photography. The latter is a form of capturing unseen things on photographic film or paper in which concentration of attention on the part of the operator is necessary for the desired results, whereas spirit forms theoretically may appear spontaneously. Experiments of this sort are conducted under various conditions also, involve differing procedures, and produce results varying in success from recognizable images of the objects upon which the experimenter had been concentrating to absolutely nothing at all. Anyone may try either type of experiment and, with a moderate expenditure for the necessary paper and film, plus time and patience, could possibly produce startling evidence of the validity of this type of phenomenon for himself.

Skotographs and its variations

During the 1940's and 1950's, one of the most famous spirit photographers of this country was a man named Jack Edwards. One of the unusual features of the work of Edwards was his willingness to work before large audiences, in moderate light, and subject to test conditions. Some of his plates were exposed in a camera in the usual manner and others were merely passed, sealed, throughout the audience in an attempt to obtain what is known as a "skotograph," a term used in spiritualist circles to designate a picture of spirits, made without the use of a camera.

In addition to this type of "skotograph" involving the use of film, there is yet another kind—that which uses only photographic paper held by individuals, each holding the paper to his own solar plexus, forehead, or simply in his hand.

SPONTANEOUS PSYCHIC PHOTOS

Since there have been spontaneous spirit photographs made, it necessarily follows that under certain conditions the camera can pick up objects which vibrate at a higher frequency than those which the human eye can detect, and the fact that some of these experiments are carried out without the use of an instrument such as a camera, makes them even more mysterious and astonishing.

One need not necessarily believe in the concepts of spiritualism in order to photograph discarnate entities. There are countless photographs of this nature, made quite unintentionally, a classic example of which was widely publicized a few years back. A family visiting an old church in England took some interior shots of a choir stall. After development, one of the exposures showed every seat in the choir section filled with distinguishable forms, clothed in the apparel of another era. The rest of the shots showed the seats empty, just as they appeared to the physical eyes of the sightseeing group. This picture will no doubt be recalled by many who read this, as this story was nationally syndicated.

Another picture which received nationwide attention was one that a couple took of their new car. When the prints were returned to them, one of the prints showed the wife's mother, deceased for some time, seated in the back of the car with a pleased smile on her face! Here again is an example of a spontaneous spirit photograph.

A dear friend of mine, recently passed away, had two snapshots which are genuine spontaneous spirit photographs; at least, they are snapshots which show faces where faces should not logically appear.

One of these is a snapshot of her husband looking over a retaining wall, and the foreground of the picture is solid and unshadowed, the flat surface of a concrete sidewalk. On the plain gray of the sidewalk are two faces, very clear and distinct. One of them they recognized as a deceased member of the family, while the other face is that of a stranger to them, but distinguishable and sharp to such a degree that it would be readily recognizable to anyone who did know the gentleman.

The second photograph is an interior shot taken at night with the use of a flashbulb. It shows two people seated on a sofa. Behind them, above eye level, is a long window rather high on the wall, and over and between the heads of the two persons on the couch is a face. It would almost appear to be the face of someone outside looking in, but there is an inhuman quality about the features. Its ugliness is almost monstrous, but neither frightening nor unpleasing—a most peculiar sight, but definitely not a face of someone in the room reflected on the glass, even allowing for the distortion which could be the cause of unrecognizability.

Both of these pictures were taken under circumstances such as one would take such snapshots, with no thought that there might appear on them any of these unseen guests. The woman who owned the pictures was one of the nicest people I have ever met; a natural but absolutely non-commercial psychic. I know that she would never stoop to fraud.

TEST CONDITIONS FOR SPIRIT PHOTOGRAPHY

Test conditions for spirit photography seances, employing the use of a psychic photographic medium, are fairly universal. They consist primarily of making sure that the film, paper, and camera or plates to be used in the experiment are never within reach of the medium or any possible confederates, prior to the actual testing. As a general rule, the supplies are held by a member of the testing committee from the time of purchase until the films have been developed and prints made in his presence.

Occasionally the films are purchased by an outsider who is not apprised of the nature of the use to which they are to be put, and in sufficient quantity to keep the manufacturer's seal on the package intact until the test is to be started.

Some testing committees are chosen immediately preceding the test, if it is being held as a group seance. Others are more or less permanent testing groups made up of researchers who are interested in gathering evidence.

The camera, if one is used, is subjected to careful examination before the exposures are made in order to preclude the possibility that tampering or malfunction might be involved in the event anything unusual appears in the finished pictures.

The film and paper to be used in the experiments are usually opened in a darkroom and marked for identification by committee members just before the tests are made.

If a medium is being tested, the lighting conditions are usually those which meet his requirements. If a photographer, other than the medium, is being employed for the test, the lighting requirements are generally suited to the medium's request, while the equipment specifications are those to suit the photographer. This is generally the case where manifestations produced by a medium are the objects of the tests, rather than the type of thing which is the aim of what is usually called psychic photography. True "spirit photographers" are mediumistic themselves and thus do not require the presence of a second sensitive, according to some theories.

Mediumship not required

By some concepts, primarily those held by spiritualists, capturing spirit presences on photographs is a special kind of mediumship, and only those who are genuine mediums can do this. There may be some truth in this claim, but if it *is* true, it must be that this is one form of psychism which is dormant in many, since there have been many "spirit extras" caught on film by those who have not the slightest knowledge of such phenomena.

I do not subscribe to the theory that this can be demonstrated only by mediums, in the spiritualistic meaning of the word "medium." It may be true that it is an ability that can be strengthened or improved with practice and by following certain prescribed procedures. However, this is true even of the commercial photographer—he, too, produces better results as he refines and understands the process of picture taking.

It is also probable that a photographer would benefit from an understanding of the spiritualist explanation of the vibrational frequency of light rays, the composition of the astral body which is hypothetically what shows in spirit photos, and some of the conditions which forerunners in the field have found to be most conducive to good results.

HOW TO PROCEED FOR SPIRIT PHOTOGRAPHY

Some experimenters insist that good results can be obtained only if infra-red film is used, because of the very high frequency of the vibration of the astral forms. This obviously is not true since many accidental or unanticipated spirit photos have been obtained with far less sensitive film. It is only when lighting conditions make the use of ordinary film implausible that the highly sensitized infra-red film is necessary or practical. For most purposes, the high-speed film used by almost all photographers, amateur or otherwise, is sensitive enough. For thought-form photography, skotographs, or any experiments which do not require a camera, one may use highly sensitive strong contrast paper.

According to spiritualistic procedure of practice and development of this ability, it is generally suggested that the attempts to capture spirit forms on film will be more fruitful if the following procedure is used:

Sympathetic environment

As a preliminary to the attempt, it is extremely beneficial to sit privately with an intimate friend who is in sympathy with your experiment. This sitting should be conducted in the same manner as any type of seance would be attempted; that is, the participants sit quietly and expectantly, in subdued light, either at a table with the hands resting lightly on the surface or with pencil and paper in hand. When and if intelligible communication begins, the communicating force should be asked if he will assist with the experiment, and that a signal be given when a photographic exposure will be successful.

When the signal is given (by raps or tilting, if the table method is used, or by writing if the automatic writing method is chosen), one of the sitters takes his place against a dark background as for an ordinary photograph. Again ask that a spirit appear on the film and that a signal be given when the shutter should be clicked.

This is the method recommended by spiritualists, and they maintain that it will be productive of results which will prove conclusively that spirits can be photographed if one has the patience to continue over a reasonable period of time.

Manifestations to recognize

The first evidence of success will probably be mere blurs or spots of light which have the appearance of defects in the film or paper. However, according to teachers of this method, the more persistent the effort, the more evidential the results will become.

By way of an aside, let me say here that there are some spiritualists who will accept as authentic only photographs with no ears visible on the heads. I don't know whether or not this is an accurate means of determining the authenticity of the spirit form, but I must say that the most convincing spirit photos I have ever seen do have this curious characteristic. I have never heard or read any explanation of this peculiarity.

It is not at all uncommon to meet with the argument that all photographs with spirit extras on them are merely thought projections which superimpose themselves on the scene being recorded. Aside from the fact that some of them *are* very likely images of persons or things which were invited to appear by concentration on them, what about those which appear without forethought? Also, if they *are* thought forms which are captured on film, isn't this, too, an enigma which would invite investigation?

If the concept that the occurrence which we call death is simply a separation of the physical matter and the spiritual is true (and this belief is growing more widespread from the scientific point of view), the animating personality forming the mental-emotional part of each of us still exists in some form, although the density of it is different from the density of the physical body from which it has been liberated. That it exists as energy or vibrational frequency is no less feasible than that it simply ceases. The burden of proof is just as great for those who feel that it ceases as it is for those who feel that consciousness survives this change.

If this animating force simply departs from the physical body, it no doubt carries with it the energy which activated it in the first place. Since energy manifests as the subtle light we call the human aura (and by this time this should be visible to all who seriously read this primer), there is no reason to conclude that it cannot be photographed, since auras *can* be captured on film.

In psychic photography, as well as in any other experimentation in the unproven, one should bear in mind that proof at this point seems discouragingly far away. What is truth or proof for one may not be so for another. In considering results of experiments in which one has not participated himself, it is well to keep in mind a remark made by Dr. Thomas J. Hudson in the preface to his book *The Law of Psychic Phenomena*, ". . . substantial progress cannot be made in science until one is ready to accord due credit to human integrity, and to give due weight to human testimony."

According to some of the researchers and experimenters in psychic photography, the best way to set about accomplishing positive results is as follows:

Obtain the most sensitive film, paper, and camera as possible, or practical. Perhaps the most satisfactory film is Eastman Kodak Company's HIR 402. This is an infra-red film, highly sensitive, which allows lighting conditions to suit even the most particular medium. This makes it necessary to use infra-red as the light source for the exposure, but this poses no great problem. According to a fine photographer I know, any heating element such as a toaster, curling iron, etc., gives sufficient infra-red rays for photography, but an electric iron is best because its element is enclosed and does not glow.

If it is at all possible, try to have a professional photographer as a participant. Because of the extreme sensitivity of the film and paper, much that is of value might be saved from defects or even destruction by mishandling.

Camera equipment

Ideally, if a camera with a quartz crystal lens can be obtained, this gives promise of the best results. These are difficult to find, but if one is fortunate enough to have such a lens he will find it extremely sensitive and productive of exceptional results. The combination of the infra-red film and the crystal lens makes it possible to capture on film the highest frequencies since the emulsion of the film is super-sensitive and, in combination with the crystal lens, makes it possible to photograph in seconds what might not have been possible in hours with more ordinary exposure implements. The more solid the object, the lower the rate of vibration; hence, to photograph the high rate of vibration of the spirit form or the aura, one must have the most rapid and sensitive equipment available. It is true that one might accidentally capture images with less sensitive apparatus, but here we are dealing with the experimental methods.

It is desirable, if at all possible, to develop films and paper as one goes along with the tests. This gives an idea of the time adjustments which might be necessary in the exposures. This poses no problem if one uses film and paper which is not damaged by exposure in red light. It is a little more inconvenient if one is using infra-red, but here is where the professional photographer is worth his weight in gold—he will know how to handle all materials while observing all safety factors.

Double exposures

One thing must be guarded against particularly—double exposures. Some cameras are so constructed that a double exposure is impossible. If this type of camera is available, by all means use it. Many of the psychic photographs I have seen have the appearance of being superimposed images through double exposure or deliberate "doctoring." Only the fact that the methods or the equipment used rendered this impossible made them acceptable as evidence.

There are many accounts of results received during the regular conduct of seances with mediums demonstrating differing phases of highly developed mediumship.

ACCOUNTS OF RESULTS

An account of the results obtained by a group of very distinguished researchers is contained in the book *Wisdom of the Gods* by H. Dennis Bradley. This group, in England, made a practice of placing photographic paper, emulsion side up, in various places throughout the seance room. The spots where the papers were placed were chosen with an eye to inaccessability to the medium and sitters; that is, under chairs, on top of high pieces of furniture, etc. The results were very gratifying since they obtained symbols and definite markings on the untouched paper. A picture section is included in Bradley's book, showing some of the results.

Another interesting and informative book about spirit photography is by Major Tom Patterson, entitled *Spirit Photography*. This book, published in England in 1965, also contains many interesting psychic photographs reproduced in a special section, in addition to many detailed descriptions of Maj. Patterson's collection of others obtained during his years of research.

One of the most interesting and evidential psychic photographs I have ever seen is owned by Dr. Pierette Austin, the distinguished Aura scientist of New York. This photo was on display at a public lecture. It is one of two taken in immediate sequence. The first photo, taken under ordinary circumstances, shows a gentleman in the front row, obviously an amputee with one leg missing. The second photo, taken with the intent to catch possible spirit "extras," shows the same group of people, in almost identical poses, but the etheric leg of the man mentioned is clearly there—*but* it casts no shadow, as does the other leg!

This is only one of a number of fine samples of psychic photography owned by this remarkable woman.

Joseph W. Donnelly, author of *Diary of a Psychic*, is also the owner of an extensive collection of spirit photos and skotographs, some of which are reproduced in his book.

THOUGHT PHOTOGRAPHY

Thought photography, a recently much-publicized phenomenon, seems to be a highly developed ability possessed by Ted Serios. Mr. Serios, the principal of many magazine and newspaper articles and a book by Dr. Eisenbud, interviewee on television programs, and the subject of research in the parapsychology department of one of our universities, has this faculty to an apparently unparalleled degree. There have been some results produced by other lesser known people, but none seem to be as fantastic or plentiful as those of Mr. Serios.

In view of the condition which seems to be necessary for Mr. Serios to induce before he can demonstrate this gift of his, there is most likely a need for both a chemical and mental change to take place within him. It is all very well to deride such a claim, but when one deals with an unknown process it is impossible to conclude justifiably that this reported need for alcohol in the system is one of personal preference only. The test to which this man is being put in the effort to understand the how and why of this particular ability may prove that this is *not* one of the real needs to produce such sensational results—but it cannot be dismissed arbitrarily simply because one does not approve of intemperance.

HOW YOU CAN TAKE THOUGHT PICTURES

The method of obtaining thought forms on paper may be as simple as having the experimenter hold sensitized paper or film, with careful observation of the light requirements of the particular emulsion thereon, against his forehead, his solar plexus, or between the palms of his hands. It is well to have the paper or film wrapped to protect it from direct contact with the skin, which might affect the emulsion of the film.

While he concentrates completely on the object he wishes to show, the paper or film should be held in place by the experimenter for at least 15 minutes, and some teachers of this method recommend that it be held in place for a half an hour. During this time, concentration must be on the object alone as completely as possible.

In the beginning it is suggested that the image projected be uncomplicated, such as rings of light, stars, or similar simple forms. It is easier to hold a clear image in the mind if it is not too intricate. With practice it is possible to project more detailed thought forms. Recognizable faces and scenes can be produced in time, with faithful practice, according to some teachers of this skill.

USE OF COLOR FILM

Now that colored film has been developed to its present degree of sensitivity, it is hoped that the time is not too distant when it will be both practical and inexpensive to experiment with it. This should prove to be interesting, if only to bolster the argument that spirit photographs originate from another dimension than the human mind. One could concentrate on a deceased person, imagine his face blue and his hair purple. If it printed in the imagined colors, this would indeed give one food for thought. But so would it if it came out in the natural and normal color too, wouldn't it?

SPIRIT PHOTOGRAPHY ON SILK

The only thing resembling color photographs that I have seen as a result of psychic work are those which are called "precipitation on silk." This is a baffling phenomenon which I hope some day to be able to observe in action. Except for the integrity and the intelligence of the people I know who have samples of this particular process, I must admit that my credulity might be somewhat strained by it.

Each sitter at a seance conducted for this specific purpose has placed before him on a table a piece of silk approximately 8x10 inches. It appears to be quite ordinary white lustrous fabric, somewhat like sateen in texture.

When the seance is over, if it is successful, numerous faces appear to have been printed on the surface of the material. Many of them are completely recognizable by those in front of whom the fabric has rested during the entire seance. During the whole process, the sitters are supposed to keep the fingertips of both hands firmly pressed on the ends of the piece of material in front of them to hold it securely in place while the images are being impressed.

I have seen faces on silk in both black and white and in color. One piece of cloth may have just natural color heads and faces, another may have them only in black and white, while yet another may have some of each.

These pictures on silk have the appearance of rubbings similar to those one may transfer by placing a sheet of paper on top of a piece of newsprint and rubbing the entire surface of it with a smooth, dull instrument. I do not mean to imply that this is the manner in which these images were applied to the fabric—common sense would tell us that this could be done only with those people whose pictures were available on newsprint.

The most completely unique image I have ever seen on fabric was a three-dimensional profile, "embossed" on white satin. It belonged to the father of a friend of mine and depicted his mother. He showed me this unusual piece one time when I was visiting my friend some months before her death.

This unusual piece was in a shadow-box type of frame, without glass over it, and had the appearance of padded and deeply embossed satin. There was no color in it, but the depth of the impression was so great that the features were clearly recognizable to those who had known the lady. He told me that he had received this piece during a seance held by a young medium who had never seen his mother, as she had been dead for many years, possibly even before the medium had been born. This, no doubt, could not properly be called psychic photography, but I am at a loss to categorize it more exactly, therefore I include it here.

DELAYED PHOTO IMPRESSION PHENOMENA

There is another unusual feature to psychic photography; frequently "extras" appear on pictures which showed no such presences at the time the pictures were printed. They appear many weeks or months *after* the picture has been processed.

It would be very strange if one called attention to the normal photograph before the appearance of the "extras," since this would be inviting the charge that one had foreknowledge that the images were forthcoming. However, these things do happen legitimately, because in the experiments which I have done, strange markings *have* occasionally put in an appearance several days after the prints were developed.

SUMMARY OF CHAPTER THIRTEEN

1. Photographic emulsion is sensitive to frequencies not visible to the human eye.
2. Spirit photography involves presence of "unseen" persons or objects on a finished picture; thought photography captures objects or persons through concentration on them specifically.
3. Spirit photographs may be produced without the use of a camera and are called skotographs.
4. Although there are mediums who are spirit photography specialists, belief in the ability to produce such pictures is not a factor since some of the finest examples have been produced spontaneously by laymen not knowledgeable of the phenomena.
5. To be considered evidential, psychic photos must be produced under test conditions as given in this chapter.
6. You do not need highly specialized equipment or materials to produce spirit photos.
7. One form of this phenomenon is called "precipitation on silk," a phenomenon in which images and likenesses appear on fabric without photo equipment.
8. Sometimes psychic images appear long after the photographic developing and printing process has been completed.

FOURTEEN

Telepathy

with Psychic Power

"Telepathy—the supposed communication of one mind with another at a distance by other than normal sensory means; thought transference." This is the definition of the phase of psychism we are about to examine in this chapter. It is much more interesting than it would seem to be from this definition—also much more apparent as a human potential than the inclusion of the word "supposed" would lead one to expect.

A LOST ARTICLE FOUND

My own interest in the phenomenon of telepathy stems from one particular afternoon in a high school psychology class. I was indignant when the teacher discredited a "mentalist" whose performance had impressed my brother and me so thoroughly the night before at a local theater. She announced in positive tones that she was going to attend the performance that evening and expose him on the spot. She had a question in mind which she was sure would baffle him and demonstrate the fakery of his claim that he could read minds and make predictions.

The question which she had in mind, and had told no one about before she asked it publicly, concerned the disappearance of a valuable gold fountain pen.

The "mind reader" picked her out as a participant in the demonstration. He told her that if she would remove the bottom drawer in her *office* desk, she would find the object about which she was concerned. In some manner it had fallen over the end of the drawer and was resting in a depression in the floor of the desk under the bottom drawer.

It was of particular interest that emphasis was placed on an office desk, since this teacher had three desks—one at home, one in her classroom and one in her office as dean of girls. Needless to say the mentalist was given no prior clue either as to the nature of the question or the occupation of the questioner, since her prime purpose was to "expose" him.

Early the next morning, before first class, the pen was found precisely where it had been said it was. This teacher earned the respect of her pupils by making a special point to tell each class that she had been in error; telepathy was the only possible explanation.

This incident, besides inspiring admiration for the teacher for her courage and sense of fairness, has no doubt been responsible in a large measure for my sustained interest in the seemingly unexplainable.

I once accepted the opinions of so many "authorities" that this was a gift, highly specialized, possessed only by a privileged few. Now I know that it can be developed by almost anyone who makes a conscientious effort. I also know that in order to retain the ability, once it manifests, one must practice it faithfully or it diminishes again.

TWO TYPES OF THOUGHT TRANSFERENCE

There are two kinds of thought transference. The first is compulsive in nature and is the less desirable because it may leave the receiver unhappy or dissatisfied. It is based upon the imposition of the will of the sender. The second is impulsive in nature and is a persuasive way which leaves the receiver undistressed. It is based upon giving the impression that the words spoken or the action taken is self-motivated.

Sales uses

Many salesmen use thought transference, either consciously or unconsciously, in their work. It is probable that a great deal of the so-called high-pressure salesmanship is really compulsive telepathy. This is the kind of technique which employs the mental "you *are* going to buy it" imposition of will. It may prove to be very effective, but it leaves the purchaser with the feeling that he has been overpowered and has made a mistake. He buys against his better judgment, and as a result may tend to avoid further contact as much as possible. It is the old story of "He who is convinced against his will, is of the same opinion still."

Empathy use is best

On the other hand, the impulsion way of selling telepathically is effective but inoffensive, since it is sent empathetically. The purchaser is left with a feeling of satisfaction that he made up his own mind.

The compulsion type of telepathy is the forceful and concentrated manner of thinking, "You *are* going to do as I wish you to do." It is simply commanding or demanding with silent willpower that someone does or says what you want.

Impulsion is the technique of thinking of yourself as the other fellow—*become* as much this other person as it is possible for you to do. Take a moment to *be* the person to whom you are sending your thought. Then when you feel this has been accomplished, send your thought out in the first person, that is, concentrate on "*I* am going to be less negative in my attitude," or "*I* know this is the best thing for me to do."

A simple case of thought transference

One evening I was at the home of some friends. I had explained to them, just as simply as the above explanation, how thought transference works.

Although I do smoke, I try not to be offensive with it and if I am in the home of friends who do not smoke, I refrain out of courtesy unless they make it plain that they have no objection. This particular home was one in which I did not smoke because my friend's parents did not particularly approve of it and it wasn't that important to me.

A few moments after I had explained the procedure for sending thoughts, I was surprised when I found myself thinking, "I would like a cigarette." I was puzzled that the thought kept recurring, because such a thing never crossed my mind ordinarily in this home. The thought persisted, however.

Finally, I became more determined; "I am going to light a cigarette" went through my mind.

As I opened my purse and took out my cigarettes, my friend's husband started to laugh—he had proven the workability of what I had just told them.

SUGGESTION FOR ACTION REQUIRED

He explained that he had started with the first thought, then switched to the second when he realized he had no way of checking on the results of sending a thought that, because of my habit of not smoking in their home, would result in no action or comment from me; the second thought was more definite and called for action on my part.

An excellent way to prove to yourself that this really works is to send a thought which requires a definite movement or verbal response. I have often proven that I can "put words into people's mouths" by having them say exactly what I was thinking. This is excellent proof.

Let me say that I regard the use of this faculty ethical only if it is not used to take unfair advantage. Although I conducted an antique business for five years, I did not use telepathy in order to make sales. I did, however, find it a handy and inoffensive way to hurry people along if they were inclined to linger too long when I had pressing matters to attend to in the office.

Simply as a matter of proving to myself that it would work under any circumstances, I did use it to conclude some sales in the shop. Each time the customer expressed his decision to purchase the articles under consideration in exactly the words I was transmitting. Perhaps my ethics in this regard might be considered extreme (particularly in view of the fact that the business failed), but nonetheless I felt strongly that I could not use this in business in good conscience. Foolish or not, this is my feeling and I must abide by it.

I feel strongly that the law of retribution works infallibly, and that, just as the good we send out is returned to us, so does that which is less than good. This is reason enough for me to seriously examine my motive for anything—thought transference not excepted. I am convinced that selfish gain or imposition of my will would surely bring me unpleasant repercussions.

ELEMENTS OF RECEPTIVITY FOR COMMUNICATION

There is an important point to keep in mind when you are practicing the development of telepathic ability. It is virtually impossible to inject a thought into another's conscious mind when that mind is preoccupied or involved in a continuous trend of thought. As with anything else, when it is full there is no room to add anything more.

The subconscious may receive the communication, but it cannot get the conscious mind to pay attention until the train of thought with which it is busy is broken by some diversionary strategy on your part. As you attempt to transfer a thought while in the presence of the target of your attempt, it is not at all difficult to break in subtly. A movement, a sound, or a touch will be sufficient. In the blank interval, at the cessation of the continuity, the penetration will take place and the impression will lodge itself in the other person's consciousness.

By the same token, when you attempt to receive thoughts, do not concentrate or allow your own thoughts to become too tightly knit, or you will not have the blank place there for the impression to slip into place.

These inserted impressions, passed from the subconscious to the conscious, are very fleeting and must be seized upon as soon as they are recognized. It is very much like a dream experience; unless details of a dream are immediately recalled and written down upon awakening, they fade in detail and reality. Learn to note immediately any thought which seems irrelevant or extraneous to what you are doing or thinking about—it may be a telepathic message from someone you know.

As you conduct tests of this nature with a fellow experimenter, or in a group, write down every impression you receive; the one you dismiss as foolish or impossible may be the one he is sending to you.

HOW TO BEGIN TELEPATHY EXPERIMENTS

The consensus with regard to the factor of distance between sender and receiver during *development* of the telepathic ability is that the participants in the experiments should start with both in the same room, but each out of line of vision of the other.

After some degree of success is attained, try it in separate rooms. When hits are scored at this distance, widen the range.

Often a person will show signs of being a good sender but have much difficulty in receiving. If this is the case he should try to develop strength to this end; if the opposite is the case, he should practice sending. It is seldom that one is proficient at both sending and receiving, but a better balance may be achieved with practice. One may never attain such a degree of success that he can become a professional performer, but anyone can increase his ability if he has the desire and the patience to persist.

A group experiment

One evening, early in my participation in telepathic experiments, it was pretty well demonstrated to me that almost anyone with the wish to do so is capable of obtaining striking results for himself.

A group of us had assembled at a friend's home to do some of the exercises recommended for telepathic development. All of us present were real novices in such work. By previous arrangement with a gentleman of considerable experience in thought transference, we were making our first attempt at sending and receiving thoughts from quite a distance. At the time of our meeting this man was in his place of business about 60 blocks from the house where we had gathered.

A telephone call to him alerted him to the time we were going to start the sending procedure. We then selected an object upon which to concentrate. As we all kept our thoughts and eyes glued to the object, we pictured the man to whom we were attempting to convey the impression. After a few minutes of this concentration, one of the women participants drew a picture of the object on a blackboard, noting aloud as she did so details such as colors, shapes, use, nature, etc.

When we completed the first object, we decided to add another just for good measure. We followed the same procedure.

The first thing we selected was a bottle filled with a soft drink; we selected this because it was standing on a coffee table in full view of all of us. The second article we "sent" was a green leaf. We all were careful that we thought of these objects with particular regard to shape and color.

After the time allotted for the sending had elapsed, the gentleman who was on the receiving end called to report that he had the strong impression that we had visualized a tree.

In view of the fact that the liquid we had been looking at was brown, considering the shape of the bottle, and adding to that the second thought of a green leaf, we figured that this was indeed beyond coincidence. When one considers the millions of possibilities for subjects of transmission, the similarity between the trunk of the tree and this bottle which would appear to be brown because of its contents, then embellished with green leaves, seems to be far beyond chance of guessing.

During the call to report his impression, the man asked the woman on the phone to think of her clothes and said he would attempt to describe how she was dressed. She had on a black taffeta skirt, very full, and a white off-the-shoulder blouse with many ruffles. He did not know what the material was by name, but said that she had on a black, stiff full skirt and a white blouse with ruffles. Another amazing demonstration!

He then suggested that we all sit quietly and try to project ourselves mentally into his place of business and see if we could get any impressions about it. We all knew that he was a jeweler but none of us had ever been in his shop.

I do not recall all the results, but I do remember three of them, one of which was my own. One woman described a taupe china clock, even to the time shown by the hands. One of the men present described a "thin yellow box," which he said was about 8x10 inches in size and was on a counter near the telephone. I described a flat plate-like object about ten inches in diameter, Wedgwood blue in color but with no white figures on it as Wedgwood usually has.

The taupe china clock was one he had in his shop for repair, and it had stopped at the time mentioned as indicated by the hands' position seen by the woman participant who had described it.

The "thin yellow box" was an 8x10 inch yellow envelope placed beside the telephone since it contained some important papers the man wanted to be sure to take home with him that night.

The blue plate-like disc I had seen was a wooden peg-board, 12 inches around, and it was painted Wedgwood blue, including the tiny nails in it which served as hangers for tiny objects used in the man's work.

We were delighted with the results and, needless to say, some of us made it our business to rush down to the shop the next day to view the scene of our triumph and to see the objects in more material form than we had seen them the night before.

THE DUNNINGER EXPERIMENTS

At about this same time, Dunninger, the famous magician and mentalist, had a television program.

One day Dunninger announced that he was going to conduct an experiment of thought transference with his viewing audience. There were six of us in my home viewing the program. All had different impressions. I had the feeling, sound, and vision of water. For a few seconds it was as if nothing else in the world existed except *water*.

The following week at broadcast time, all of us who had seen the program at my home the preceding week, along with a number of others who had seen it elsewhere, were at a party. As we waited for the time when the results of the experiment would be announced, each of us told what our impression had been. I was the lone hold-out for water. You may well imagine how delighted I was to hear the announcement that the word had indeed been water.

NECESSITY FOR MENTAL STIMULATION

Many books and periodicals dealing with accounts of telepathic experiences seem to be involved predominantly with situations concerning crises, such as accidents, death, or serious illness. The preponderance of such incidents would almost lead one into the trap of believing that this faculty is in evidence only in times of stress.

It does seem that there is an increase of successful transference when the emotions or senses are aroused. For example, it appears that failure to attain high accuracy in scientific tests by usually skilled mentalists may be due to the lack of stimulation from the geometric symbols used in the card tests. This is certainly a perfectly reasonable assumption, since it is known that boredom or fatigue cause a noticeable diminution of receptivity—and what stimulation or interest can be aroused by repetition of geometric symbols over and over?

An acquaintance of mine recently told me that his children had responded phenomenally to a deck of cards marked with pictures of toys in color, while they were notably unsuccessful with the black and white symbols on the scientifically approved deck. Because the emotions were stimulated, the responses were more often accurate and the interest sustained over a far greater period of time.

In tests in which I have been involved, we have found that emotion and sensation *are* important factors. We have had much success when colored pictures (such as one finds in magazines) were studied by the sender, while the receiver either sat in the same room with his back turned to the sender, or sat in an adjoining room.

The most astounding score of hits in the use of regular playing cards was obtained by a woman in our experimental group, while she was under hypnotic trance. Prior to the induction of the trance she was taken through several runs with an average score, but while under hypnotic control her score averaged a fraction over 90 percent accuracy.

Sometimes as I listen to lectures, I try to anticipate the exact phrase or sentence the speaker will use. It is uncanny how frequently one can correctly pick up the right words, and, significantly, the degree of success varies with different speakers. There have been speakers I have found it impossible to anticipate, while others can be counted on to use the expected words with startling consistency.

METHODS FOR THOUGHT TRANSFERENCE

There are numerous ways one can work to develop the ability to transfer thoughts, some requiring props and others not. I shall describe in some detail a few of the most effective exercises and experiments with examples of results, in order to illustrate how one may consider or estimate the degree of accuracy.

1. Two or more may participate in this, as in most of the other exercises or experiments. Have one person, as sender, sit alone in a separate room or, at least, out of sight of the receivers. The sender should have either pencil and paper or a blackboard and chalk. As soon as he has determined what it is he wishes to draw, he gives the signal to the receivers and starts drawing. Artistic ability doesn't count—the important thing is that he *feels* what he is drawing, with as many of the five senses involved as possible. For instance, let us suppose that the sender has chosen to test with the thought of a cup of coffee. As he draws the picture, however crudely, he thinks of it in every sensory way as well as its physical aspects. He smells it, tastes it, feels the heat, the liquid quality, the color, the sensation of swallowing it, the texture and weight of the cup, the sound of it being poured into the cup, etc. In fact, he concentrates on it as a reality which he is handling, tasting, smelling, etc.

As soon as he has finished with his drawing, he puts the drawing instrument down and sits quietly for two or three minutes, still thinking of the object he is trying to send. He then signals to the receivers that he has finished.

During the time of the sending, the receivers sit quietly as they wait for impressions to come to them. They are to be equipped with pencils and paper in advance of the test so that they may jot down the impressions they receive. It is important that they understand that they are to note *every* impression they have during the test. Each receiver acts independently of the others with no comparison of thoughts until the test is concluded.

In the evaluation of results one must take into consideration each attribute of a cup of coffee. A point must be granted for each one that is noted correctly. For instance, one might mention heat, brown, and a feeling of swallowing something. Another might mention a smooth bowl filled with hot liquid along with the sound of fluid being poured. All of these apply to a cup of coffee and must be considered significant, even though no one might mention a cup of coffee specifically.

In this test, as with many of the others, the number of objects from which one might select makes it next to impossible to calculate accurately the percentage of accuracy. It is nonetheless possible to prove that telepathy has been practiced successfully.

2. This experiment is conducted in the same manner as the first one, except that the sender has available to him a number of objects, preselected and known to the receivers. He handles and concentrates on them in any order he chooses. He calls out "one" and handles the first one, "two" as he works with the second, and so on until he has handled each object at least three times in random order. It is a good idea to limit the number of objects to five. In this way it is easy to figure the percentage of accuracy of each receiver who has noted down his answers, as there are only fifteen possible correct answers. Also, this requires a short enough time that fatigue and boredom will not set in before all participants have the opportunity to send.

3. This is the experiment previously referred to which involves the use of colored pictures. One may use either the whole magazine with the choice of picture left entirely to the sender, or five or ten may be preselected for the sender to concentrate on in turn as he chooses. The latter makes it more convenient to evaluate the results.

The sender attempts to project not only the image of the picture he is using, but he also tries to convey the emotional and sensory effect of the picture. Let us suppose it is a quiet country scene, perhaps a lake, a boat, a mountain in the background, and a forest campsite in the foreground. The tranquility, coolness, distance and height (suggested by the mountain in the background), and any other emotion suggested by the mind of the sender and sensed by the receivers is evidence of telepathy. It is extremely improbable that one can devise an accurate method of scoring, but if the experiment is successful the results will be unmistakable.

4. This experiment may be conducted with all of the participants in the same room. Place eight or ten articles on a table, select one person to be the receiver and, without his knowledge, the rest of the group selects one object upon which they will all concentrate. Let the receiver then pass his hand slowly over the line of articles on the table, while the group *wills* him to find the proper one, which they keep in mind during the entire test. Watch carefully for a dip or rise of his hand as he passed his hand over the selected article. He should make at least eight passes over the full length of the line of objects. If he is receiving the impression properly his hand will repeat a noticeable break in the pattern of motion as his hand passes over the target. A series of playing cards may be used, face up on the table, but again it seems fairly evident from our experience that items stimulating to the emotions and senses are more effective.

5. Here is an interesting experiment for two people to conduct, and repeated use constitutes an effective development exercise:

Agree upon a ten minute interval which is mutually convenient and normally quiet and uninterrupted. During the first five minutes #1 acts as sender and #2 acts as receiver; in the second interval #2 sends while #1 receives.

Agree upon general areas of subject matter—for instance, a friend and I who practiced this would send three thoughts each—a quotation, the clothes we were wearing at the time of the test, and what activity we deliberately pursued during the test.

Each of us, during her time of sending, would spend the first two minutes thinking intently and repetitiously about a familiar quotation. Then for a minute we would concentrate on the clothes worn at the time. The activity of the last two minutes would be a simple but specific one, such as combing the hair, washing the hands, drumming the fingers—anything definite which could be repeated or continued for the two minutes involved.

Each made notes of impressions received during the sending time of the other, and at the end of the ten minute interval we would check with each other by telephone. We found that as we practiced we achieved greater rapport, achieving highly accurate results during the test times, but even more interesting—we found that we could effectively make mental contact with each other at times which were not predetermined.

6. Another group experiment: Have one person act as sender. He tells a story, leaving out certain details as he relates the experience. As he comes to the point in the story where he is going to visualize rather than describe aloud the activity or object he has chosen, he pauses and *thinks* as clearly as he can of the omitted facts. During the silent period, while the sender mentally sends the impressions, the receivers write down the ideas they seem to receive from the sender's mind.

Thought transference of imaginary situations

The sender should try to make his story one which involves purely imaginary places and activities. He should not draw on his own experiences or local sites. *This precludes the tendency to reason and rationalize on the part of the receivers.* For example, the sender should visualize himself walking down an imaginary street, looking in imaginary shop windows, dining in an imaginary restaurant, and so on.

The sender should use his imagination freely and leave out only those details (in narrating his "trip") which he can vividly picture in his own mind. He might, for example, describe a visit to a restaurant and, as he enters the foyer, his attention is caught by something unusual. He then concentrates silently on a lighting fixture, fountain, or anything unusual in detail which he can picture mentally and vividly. After about 30 seconds of concentration, he resumes his story orally, proceeding into the dining room, and is conducted to a table where he takes note of a centerpiece, perhaps; again he leaves out the details, preceding his thought projection with the simple statement that he has noticed the centerpiece. If he has pictured in his mind a centerpiece of flowers with a few candles placed in the arrangement, he thinks of the colors, fragrance, names, flames, etc. Following this he may mention that he hears an orchestra playing in the background, then sits quietly while he mentally sings the tune he hears. He orders food, but does not tell what it is—he mentally *eats* whatever it is he has ordered.

Once again, it is important in selecting the objects or activities that those which have the strongest sensory or emotional appeal be chosen. It is surprising how accurately these projections can be picked up by the receivers.

In this experiment it is well to limit the number of projections to five for each sender.

7. One more suggestion, although the ideas for tests are innumerable. In a group test, hand out copies of lists, prepared in advance, to everyone but the receiver in each test. These lists may be made out well in advance of the tests—in this way it is possible for more than one to serve as receiver if more than one set of test lists is prepared. Each sender is given a copy of the same list for each test, of course; each test requires a new series of items on the lists.

There should be five items on each set of lists, said items numbered from one to five in sequence. Each of the five words should be representative of something which will stimulate one of the five senses; that is, (1) Red (sight), (2) Roses (smell), (3) Satin (touch), (4) Thunder (hearing), (5) Vinegar (taste).

As each number is called, all of the senders concentrate on the proper word and the emotional or sensory reaction to it. The receiver may give his impressions orally and as soon as he feels he has received all he can from the impressions sent, the next word is projected. On numerous occasions I have seen all five words properly named and in correct order. One woman participant could get them all correct but usually received nothing from the first projection, staying one number behind throughout. This is called displacement, a term used particularly in card tests when the sequence is incorrect although only in that the inaccuracy is one of either delayed or preguessed relationship to the proper number on the list.

Some of these tests are of practically no scientific value since they do not lend themselves to mathematical precision in scoring. Nevertheless, it is in tests such as these that the individual can prove to his own satisfaction that he, too, is telepathic. More scientific tests may follow these if one is really interested in the proof of telepathic ability on a more exacting basis.

Telepathy can be very useful. I know of two wives who "reformed" their husbands without nagging. One mentally convinced her husband that he wanted to give up cigars, after years of fruitless discussion and dissension about his inability to stop smoking, despite his repeated declaration that he wanted to do so. The other woman had an inveterate poker-playing husband, who consistently lost more money than they could afford. A few mental treatments and her spouse stayed contentedly at home on poker nights, completely convinced that he had "seen the light" and given up his expensive habit by his own decision and good judgment.

A question of ethics, or invasion of privacy? Perhaps, but not many husbands receive relief from painful situations in such a painless manner!

SUMMARY OF CHAPTER FOURTEEN

1. Telepathy will work in varying degrees for anyone.
2. Practice develops the ability, and continued use keeps it active.
3. There are two kinds of thought transference—compulsive and impulsive—the latter more effective and desirable.
4. Thoughts can only be received when the target is not involved in concentration on a train of thought.
5. Although distance is not an important factor in well-developed transference, it is best to practice initially on persons in the same room, increasing distance as the success increases.

6. Generally speaking, it is rare that anyone excels at both sending and receiving; it is usual to be markedly better at one than the other.
7. It seems that an emotional factor increases success at first, so use emotion-stimulating thoughts or objects in practice.
8. There are numerous exercises and experiments to use for the development of this psychic faculty, some of which are included in this chapter.

FIFTEEN

Miscellaneous

Types of Psychic

Power and Phenomena

In the broad sense of the words "psychic phenomena," there are so many classifications and sub-classifications that it is necessary to include miscellaneous phenomena too difficult to allocate under specific headings, but too important to ignore in this book.

For example, how do we classify strange and unexplained disappearances? Or the psychic abilities of some animals? Or the experiences of the persons who "return from the dead"? Or "fourth dimension" incidents? Space phenomena? Stigmatists? Unseen guidance?

"UNEXPLAINED" DIFFERENCES

Strange and unexplained disappearances have always excited the imagination. I do not refer to those which involve people who drop from sight voluntarily, nor to those about which there is reason to suspect foul play even though there is no corpse to prove it. I mean those curious stories where a man, woman or child seems to evaporate before the startled eyes of witnesses.

Equally intriguing are the stories concerned with the mystifying disappearance of whole ships, such as the "Iron Mountain" in 1872, and the "Mississippi Queen" in 1873. Or the disappearance of entire buildings, such as the story of a barn which vanished in April of 1955. The books of Frank Edwards provide what may well be the richest treasure trove of these mysteries—brief accounts, lacking in detail, probably because there was not too much that could be said except that in the presence of witnesses these things were there one moment and gone the next.

One such incident occurred on December 5, 1945, just off the east coast of Florida. It received nationwide coverage in the news media since it concerned the disappearance of *six* planes—five Avenger torpedo bombers from the Naval Air Station at Fort Lauderdale and a giant Martin Mariner sent out to search for the missing Avengers! After a search unequalled in history, a naval board of inquiry announced that there was absolutely no sign of any of the planes or crew members, no debris, in fact, nothing but an unbelievable case of six planes and their crews vanishing completely from the same general area within a matter of hours. This story has no conclusive ending—except that it is officially classified as totally unexplainable!

Some years ago I bought a book about UFO's, and I remember that it was liberally laced with stories of strange disappearances which the author contended could possibly be attributed to "space kidnappers."

One of these stories stood out vividly enough that I never quite forgot the feeling of horror I felt when I read it. It concerned the disappearance of a young man—right from the yard of his own home. There was a light snow on the ground on this particular night. The young man's parents were having a party in honor of their son and his fiancèe. Around midnight the young man's mother asked him to go out to the well for some water. Taking a bucket and a lantern he went out into the yard. In a moment the guests were startled to hear shouts for help coming from the yard. Almost in a body they rushed outside to investigate. They could hear the youth's voice calling desperately for help from the dark sky over the spot where his footsteps ended in the snow. The bucket and lantern came tumbling down from above, but there was never a trace found of the young man—he had simply vanished from the face of the earth!

A classic story in this category, recorded in so many books and periodicals that I mention it only briefly here, is the story of the strange disappearance of a man named David Lang. He was walking across an open space between his farm fields and his home in Gallatin, Tennessee, in full view of his wife, children, and some men who had come to see him on business. While they were all watching him approach, in broad daylight, he simply seemed to dissolve, leaving no trace. An exhaustive search was made of the field where Mr. Lang was last seen—experts were called in to look for sink-holes, etc., and the entire area eventually was completely dug up—to no avail. Mr. Lang was never heard from or seen again!

Stories of this sort may be found in almost any collection of true but incredible mysteries. Because of the nature of the circumstances involved, some of them fall into the category of the supernatural or super-normal. No doubt many who read them are inclined to discount the reports as inaccurate, exaggerated or purely fictional. This is the lazy and unrealistic approach—it is always easier to say something never happened than it is to explain "how" and "why." Too many of these cases have been carefully documented and witnessed to be so lightly dismissed, and psychism may well furnish the explanation.

Psychic abilities of animals

As far as the psychic abilities of animals is concerned, I am sure that anyone who has ever had a pet has observed the sixth sense so many animals possess. This is such a common attribute that it is generally accepted as a matter of course. Unless the animal concerned exhibits some almost unbelievable accomplishment, we hear very little about it.

What is it that accounts for the precognitive ability so often demonstrated by animals and birds? What caused the birds to leave the earthquake area many hours before the terrible disaster struck the Lake Hebegan district in Montana in August, 1959? No one has ever figured the "how" in the accounts of the ability of Jim, the English setter, to make accurate predictions time after time before his death in Sedalia, Missouri, in 1937.

The list of books and periodicals which contain reports of stories of this nature is much too voluminous to include here, but the subject is well worth looking into if one is interested in the topic. It is not my purpose to retell stories that have already been told, and any to which I have referred are included only to make a point clear. I have read accounts of psychic ants, snakes, flies, birds, and almost any kind of animal one could name.

My personal experience with super-sensitive animals seems to be largely limited to cats, with one exception, probably because they happen to be my favorite animals and I have had more of them than any other.

Only one who has had pets who were much loved members of the family will understand the deep sorrow and regret behind the following story:

Some years ago, because circumstances made it necessary to do so, my daughter and I had the heart-breaking task of disposing of our two cats. The mother cat, a lovely blue Maltese with a snow-white bib (from which we arrived at the name of "Bibber" for her), had been a pampered member of our family for about 13 years. The other cat was her only "child"—a personality-crammed cat called "Freddie," short for Frederica. Both of these cats were house pets—they were never allowed to go outside. Freddie was about three years younger than her mother and had been born on a Palm Sunday morning on the foot of my bed.

My daughter had moved to New York and I was moving into one room. We had to provide the best possible arrangements for our two wonderful cats. I could not bring myself to take them to the Humane Society, but we felt that it would be less cruel to have them put to sleep than to uproot them from the only home they had ever known, even if we had been able to find homes for them.

Sick at heart because no other solution could be found, I finally agreed to let a member of the family who understood how difficult it would have been for me to do it take the old friends out to have them put to sleep.

The two cats had been left in the locked house that had been their home for so many years. When the time came to pick them up, Freddie was gone! She had vanished from that locked house!

Months passed. Then one day, Freddie was found in the utility room of the house in which I was staying. To my knowledge she had never been in that house, but she no doubt either saw or heard me or my car, which stood in the street in front of the house. Except for being somewhat thinner than she had been, she was the same delightful character she had been previously. I don't know when I have been so moved by any experience as this one. Our reunion was one of the highlights of my life.

I was, by this time, due to another set of unexpected circumstances, almost ready to move back into my old home and had been very sorry many times that I had disposed of these two old friends. Now, just when I had a home to offer her again, Freddie turned up!

This story is included, not for the emotions of the humans involved, but for the mysterious way that Freddie sensed danger, stayed hidden for months and then came back at just the right time to pick up life again in her old home.

Psychic reactions of dogs

What is it that dogs react to when they bristle and growl at things we do not see or hear? Why is it that they seem to sense the presence of family members who have passed away? What is it that makes them sense impending death? There has to be something that is beyond our comprehension, or at least beyond our human senses at the present stage of our development. There are too many accounts to dismiss these stories lightly. Could it be a sixth sense that man has lost through disuse?

Some years ago my parents were going away for several weeks and asked us to stay on the grounds of the place where my father was employed. Insurance laws required that someone be in residence at all times. My daughter, her father, and I moved in, along with our dog; the bedrooms were in a second floor wing which had eight bedrooms and numerous baths, closets, and two stairways to the ground floor.

Our first indication that there was anything strange in the atmosphere was the flat refusal of the dog to go up the stairs. After much cajoling and firm orders, the dog finally, with obvious reluctance, crept up the stairs. His terror was unmistakable, and before we knew it he was back downstairs. He just *would not stay*, no matter who was with him.

That night, after we went upstairs to go to bed, we heard footsteps on the third floor. A thorough search of every nook and cranny of the entire wing showed that no one was there but the three of us and the thoroughly frightened dog, now on a leash. After a restless night, undisturbed except for the dog's nervousness, we were all glad to go downstairs and take up our daily routines.

After my husband had gone off to his work, I went upstairs to make the beds. I was surprised to find the door to my husband's room locked. I couldn't imagine why he had done such a thing, but made up the other beds and forgot about the locked door.

That afternoon, when he came home, my husband announced that he was going up to shower and shave and get ready for the evening. In a few minutes he was back downstairs. He wanted to know why I had locked his door and what I had done with the key!

It turned out that neither of us had even seen a key, but each assumed that the other had. We searched for hours and finally, in order to get into the room, we had to resort to measures which almost destroyed the door.

Thus began ten days of the most unnerving harassment I have ever experienced. Locked doors were unlocked, unlocked doors were locked. Water would appear on surfaces where it should not logically be. Strange sounds would startle us at all hours of the day and night. Through it all, the dog was the only one who could *see* what was happening, as these things took place. He was not ordinarily a fearful or cowardly dog—he was a happy-natured companionable mixture of setter and spaniel. This ten-day interlude, I am sure, was the most dreadful time he had ever spent in his fairly long life.

In considering the possibilities of this case, in view of the fact that my parents lived undisturbed in this place for about six years, it seemed to me that the explanation must have been concerned primarily with the dog. Could it be that his fear stemmed from the fact that whatever the source of the mysterious activity it was set off by resentment of the dog's presence? He seemed to be the one who suffered most acutely and continuously. We were annoyed, but he was terrified.

Two of my widowed friends have dogs, old members of their families, who many times seem to have acted as if they saw their masters present in the houses.

One of the women told me that her dog, for many months after her husband passed away, went through the motions of greeting his master at the door, excitedly wagging his tail, and trotting around the house as if following someone. Her husband's working hours had been erratic because of the nature of his business, so it could not have been a time habit. Several times the dog even jumped on the bed that had been the master's and went through the motions of licking her husband's face, as he had done so often during her husband's lifetime.

Although the other friend was widowed before I met her, I have frequently seen her dog, now very old, sit at her husband's place at the dining table, and act as if his master was there. He has also, upon a number of occasions, become unaccountably excited and behaved as if he were aware of a presence we could not see.

Habit or imagination seem to me to be a far less reasonable explanation than that they have the ability to see what we cannot see. The refinement of man's reasoning mind has weakened considerably his intuitive attributes. This is not an original or exclusive conclusion. Nor do I mean to imply that it is unfortunate that man has developed his intellectual powers, but it is a pity that he has so neglected his psychic capacity. I am sure that these two could exist together on an amicable basis.

Death-bed utterances

The increase of interest in death-bed utterances is an encouraging sign that there is more general recognition of the possibility that this is not necessarily the raving of delirium. The reported words of some of the dying are indications that there are presences around us which we do not see under more ordinary circumstances. It may be that animals are more sensitive to these presences than man is, and it is this sensitivity which accounts for their otherwise unexplainable actions.

CREDIBILTY OF REPORTED PSYCHIC EXPERIENCES

I am not unaware of the traps into which people often stumble because of an eagerness to believe that which they would like to believe. It is true that some of the stories related by persons who have presumably returned from the dead may be sheer fabrications, invented for dramatic effect. This is true in every phase of the unprovable, whether it is in the field of the psychic, investment, or politics. You name the field and you can find a fraud. But the fact still remains that there are enough accounts on record, even in that aristocrat of psychical periodicals, *The International Journal of Parapsychology*, to lend an aura of believability to the concept that the consciousness does continue after death.

Experiences preceding death

Within my own family there was an occurrence of a most interesting nature preceding death. Also, twice during critical illnesses, my
own father reported interesting experiences of such a nature as to
indicate that death is not much different from life as we know it.

What makes these particular episodes significant to me is that
neither of the persons involved had any but the most orthodox views
concerning death, had ever showed any interest in the question of
survival of the personality, or had any information in their backgrounds upon which to draw to make their experiences coincide
with others of a similar nature.

The episode preceding death involved an aunt who seemed to
wander back and forth between this world and the next for many
hours before she passed away. During the lingering last stages, she
reported, while in a perfectly calm and rational state, that she had
seen various family members who had long been gone (including a
son and her husband), and announced that she was going to join
them for Christmas. In times of non-lucidity, she talked in an intelligent manner with various family members who seemed to be
waiting for her to come to their side of life.

There was no pain or fear in this illness. She had lived her allotted
70 years, with an extra 20 thrown in for good measure, and she had
simply worn out. Here was no wishful thinking, no delirium. The
only confusion which she evidenced was an uncertainty about
which side of life the nurse in attendance was in—she recognized
everyone in her family when they were at her side, but the nurse
was someone she had not known in life and so was uncertain about
where she belonged.

I do not say that this constitutes proof that discarnate entities
were there in the room with her, but I do say that the burden of
proof rests as strongly on the shoulders of those who disbelieve it as
on those who accept it.

The other two instances to which I referred, involving my father,
both took place in my presence. Although my entire adult life has
been devoted to little that did not in some way involve the esoteric,
I am the only member of my immediate family with such an interest. There were never discussions about such things as life after

death, communication, or psychic experiences within my family circle. Because of this fact I find the two following stories of particular interest.

The first instance occurred a number of years ago during an illness which was so critical that my father was not left alone for more than a moment or two at a time. One afternoon, for no apparent reason, my father asked who the people were who had been in his room earlier that afternoon. Except for my mother, my brother and me there had been no one in the house during that period about which he inquired. He described a man and a woman, whom he said he did not know, but said that they were very pleasant and stood at the foot of his bed for some time. He felt quite calm about their visit, seemed reassured and peaceful about it, even when we told him that there had been no one in his room. This was not unlike the many reports I have read of the presence of guardian spirits who give aid and comfort during times of crisis. It was a very real experience for my father, one which was beyond his comprehension, yet he accepted it as perfectly normal.

The second incident was somewhat different. My dad had been pronounced incurably ill with cancer—it was in its terminal stage when we brought him home from the hospital. Five doctors on the case concurred in the statement that he could not possibly live more than five days after we brought him home.

One of the doctors on the case had been our family physician for many years. He knew that I had been trained in the use of hypnosis and when I asked if he would give me permission to use it on my father he told me to go ahead—he would assume full responsibility. He explained that constant narcosis had so weakened my father's heart that further injections would be increasingly dangerous; if I could keep him comfortable without drugs, it would be most beneficial. I told the doctor that it was my intention to *heal* him, not just make him comfortable.

I worked constantly for almost 12 hours—never leaving the bedside; then I worked almost constantly for another eight hours, leaving the room for only minutes at a time. Each time he would begin to stir or make a sound I would immediately start talking to him. As the benefits of the trance state built up, I could leave his bedside for longer periods of time until, after 48 hours, he slept for long enough periods so that I could sleep myself.

On the tenth day he was out of bed, shaved himself, and had a meal at the table with the family. He never mentioned the following after he was up and about, but he did tell me about it the day he had the experience:

About the fifth day after I had begun treating him, he had started to regain strength, could stay awake without discomfort, and could converse for a few minutes at a time with family members. I was in the room with him when he roused, recognized me and spoke to me in a perfectly rational, normal way. He told me that he had been with his mother and a brother who had been gone for many years. He had suffered so much that he wanted to stay with them. In an almost hurt tone of voice, he said that they had told him he must come back—it was not yet time for him to join them permanently. They had explained to him they would be waiting for him when it was right for him to come later to be with them. He said it was wonderful to be with them—he didn't know *where* he had been, but he was positive that it was a real place and that his mother and brother were actually living there.

The above took place six years before he did go to stay with them (a year and a half ago at the time of this writing), this time permanently as the result of a fatal heart attack. The cancer was entirely gone during the intervening years, during which time the "visit" with his mother was not discussed, but it completely removed his fear of death (if he had any) for he knew what it was like.

I know of one other case of this nature—regarding the utterances of the dying. This death occurred before I had any acquaintance with the family, but the deceased had been the husband of a friend of mine. She said that just before her husband died, he said clearly and unmistakably, "This country has not been kind to me. I am going back to France again." This sounds as though a recall of past lives might possibly have been taking place, since this man had never been in France during this lifetime.

Awareness of impending death

In my files I have a clipping from a newspaper from Ceylon. It was brought to me by some friends who came to this country from there several years ago. It was a report of a seance in London, which purportedly was visited by the spirit of H. Dennis Bradley, author of *Wisdom of the Gods*. Mr. Bradley's son is quoted in the article as having said that the material produced in the seance, which he attended, was evidential of his father's presence.

One of the questions in the article concerned the state of consciousness at the time of death—at what time was Mr. Bradley aware of actually dying, and did he have any glimpses of where he was going before actual death took place?

The reply was that he had had glimpses before he died, and the spirit of Mr. Bradley quoted a remark he had made on his deathbed about how wonderful it was. This does not *prove* communication is a reality, nor that the deathbed experience was *really* as reported in this seance, but it certainly is an interesting and apparently satisfactory (to Mr. Bradley's son) comment on perception at the time of death.

I can accept that there are vistas and entities beyond, which can and may be revealed to us before we die, if we can accept the possibility that it can happen. Here again we are faced with something just as difficult to disprove as it is to prove. Is it not possible that these beings are inhabitants of the fourth dimension? And is it not equally possible that we may, in certain states of consciousness, visit that dimension? It does not seem any more strange to me than having a dream come true.

THE FOURTH DIMENSION

This mysterious something, called the fourth dimension, is the setting for many strange experiences reported in apparent good faith by sensible, down-to-earth people from every walk of life. Proof of these experiences is especially difficult as there are rarely witnesses. There have been a few cases where more than one person shared in what seemed to have been an excursion into this sphere where time and place do not exist as we know them. Many reports on this type of incident have appeared in print in periodicals and anthologies of unusual occurrences, as well as in serious research works.

Most of the descriptions of these episodes imply that the time is the past—indicated by the costumes of the people seen during the adventures or by the significance of the action. Of such nature is the encounter described by Sir Cecil E. Denny in his book, *Rider of the Plains*. He had this experience while he was serving as an officer in the early days of the Northwest Mounted Police.

Considerably fewer of the anecdotes recorded are involved with impending events, possibly because these are considered to be precognitive experiences and are so classified.

Many prominent men of the past have made efforts to devise some means of selecting vibrations of past events out of the vastness of "space" around us. Men such as Thomas Edison believed that events have no ending—the vibrations travel on and on into infinity.

A camera has been devised and extensively tested which records the vibrational "residue" of objects long after the objects themselves have been displaced. According to newspaper and magazine reports, this camera was tested by the United States Armed Forces in Miami, Florida, among other spots. Several pictures were printed at about the same time of parking lots, long empty when the photographs were taken, showing images of cars that had been parked in them earlier in the day.

We are nearing proof of the fourth dimensional world. If inanimate objects leave their marks on their surroundings, how much more logical to believe that living persons would do the same!

Discarnate manifestation in fourth dimension

It does not seem illogical in this light to believe that discarnates, through the consciousness which activated them in the first place, could produce much activity that could mysteriously stimulate the physical senses of the living. Nor does it seem too unlikely that some of the "hauntings" might just be the lingering vibrations of past residents, now living elsewhere in the flesh but still inhabiting the former location in the vibrational "residue" sense.

PSYCHIC CHILDREN

This seems to be about as good a place as any to bring up the subject of psychic children. It is an accepted fact that children are frequently known to have imaginary playmates. How imaginary are they, really? Isn't it possible that the innate instincts of the so-called lesser forms of animal life are also present in man? Could it not be that children, at their early stage of expression before the process of intellectual conformity is foisted upon them, might possibly exercise the sixth sense we hear so much about?

A child's experience with a psychic companion

I have heard many first-hand accounts of children with invisible companions, but one stood out because it had rather sinister overtones. It was told to me in complete sincerity and I am as sure that it is true as if it had happened to my own child. The mother of the child concerned in this story has since passed away, but she was a friend whose honesty and intelligence were unquestionable. Fantastic as this story sounds, I can accept it as true and unexaggerated.

The boy in this story is now a young man who made a name for himself in the field of sports during his school years.

In the first few years of his life, he was an average healthy youngster. Then the father's work took them out of the country and for a time the child was rather lonely because of the language barrier. They lived, the parents and their only child, in an upper floor apartment, which was the scene of this dramatic story. Although they did not know it at the time they moved in, the parents were later told that a little boy had been killed in a fall from a tree in the back yard some months prior to the time they moved there. The apartment in which they lived had been this child's home.

Some weeks passed and the parents noticed that their boy had acquired an imaginary playmate with whom he played games, carried on conversations, and in every other way enjoyed the companionship of a child the parents could not see. This is not too unusual, so the parents were not disturbed about it. Children have been known to play this way with animals, grown-ups or children of their "imagination" for hundreds of years; there is no stigma attached to this kind of association, and youngsters outgrow this sort of thing in time.

As time passed, in this case, however, the parents became concerned for their child's health as one serious illness followed hard on the heels of another. The general well-being of the boy declined more with each illness, and his attitude toward his playmate became less carefree.

One day, while the boy was in bed because the most recent illness had been a long one which sapped his strength, the mother overheard her boy arguing with the unseen child. Her son was insisting that he preferred staying with his parents to going away with his playmate. The argument was heated on her child's part and he ended it by ordering the other child to go away and not come back.

The parents were convinced that this friendship had been one with the spirit of the child who had been killed in the fall from the tree. They felt that the illness had been induced to bring about a permanent relationship the dead child was trying to effect. This argument which the mother overheard was the end of the contact between the two boys.

After convalescing from this last of a long series of illnesses, her child once again became the normal, healthy and active child he had been, with no more invisible friends.

This may seem like an imaginative tale, but I am convinced that it was not. There are countless other reports of somewhat similar nature. I have two other friends who told me of their children's invisible playmates, but neither had the undesirable side effects of the one above.

A little girl's psychic companion

One of these concerned an unknown invisible; at least there was no recognizable connection between the little girl and her unseen companion. Nevertheless, this little girl loved her friend dearly and included him in every game, treat or trip which she experienced herself. The mother told me that her daughter insisted that the family wait for him if he happened to be a little slow about getting ready to go somewhere with them, room had to be left for him in the car, doors had to be held open so he would not get caught in them, etc. The rest of the family made sort of a game out of it without teasing her, but it was a serious matter to the little girl.

A first-hand experience with psychic companions

Another story was told to me by a woman who had experienced this herself as a child. This story concerned the death of a real little boy who had been a playmate, a little boy of her own age. He continued to romp and play with her and a few of the other children after his death.

She said she could distinctly remember arguing with her mother that the child was not in the casket on the day of his funeral because she and the other children played with him in the yard during the services.

Months passed. The parents of the little girl were naturally concerned when she continued to insist that the boy had not left at all; he joined her and the other children at play, and she frequently talked with him.

Finally her parents took her to see the family doctor; they were sure that the loss of her playmate had affected her reason in some way. The doctor must have been a most unusual man, for he assured her parents that their little girl was perfectly sane and sound. He explained to them that it is not unusual for children to be much more aware of the "unknown" than grown-ups are. What a wise man he must have been! Time took care of separating the children, but the doctor averted what might have been an emotional disaster by counseling the parents wisely.

Children outgrow these playmates, just as they outgrow others, if parents will be patient and reasonable in their approach to these situations. Who is to say that imagination is actually the explanation? Young children are known to have lively and startling flights of fancy, but what is the origin of them if they have not been told such stories upon which to base their own? There are too many cases where no such experiences have been believed or discussed in the child's presence, to make acting or copying reasonable explanations either.

As Francis Bacon said, "If we begin with certainties, we shall end in doubt; but if we begin with doubts, we shall end in certainties." Certainly this is true in the area of phenomena—one may have theories, tentative beliefs, or possible conclusions, but until proof positive is found one must stand always ready to modify or amend one's concepts. To do otherwise is to limit enlightenment. A mind closed to any but its own predetermined ideas can move only toward stagnation, resulting in bigotry or fanaticism.

A CORRECT ATTITUDE FOR DOUBT

There are two kinds of doubt. One is the kind that implies that whatever is being doubted is a complete impossibility. With this attitude manifest, rationalization and discussion are a waste of time.

The other kind of doubt, a much more healthy attitude, implies that the whole thing is improbable, but if truth *is* there for anyone, it may reveal itself to all who will take the time and effort to look and listen.

I have seen both kinds of doubt portrayed on the faces of people to whom I have told the story of the day it rained frogs when I was 11 years old. I am sure that if I were to say that I doubted the existence of South America simply because I have not seen it, I would be met with pitying or condescending looks—even from the people who really feel justified in doubting that it can rain frogs, simply because they have not seen it do so. But these frogs were just as real as the continent of South America, and hundreds of people saw them fall from the sky until they literally blanketed a large area of the city.

Ice falls, stone showers, rains made up of red sand, seeds, dried leaves, fish, blood, worms, ladybirds, and unidentifiable substances compared to butter, spider, webs, felt and many other things—fell from the sky like rain, all reported in *The Books of Charles Fort,* recommended reading for those who do not have closed minds. It might even reactivate some of these if they could be persuaded to read this book in its entirety.

To doubt an established fact is foolhardy; when sufficient evidence has been presented to prove actuality of an event or condition, only the most fanatical mind can deny the reality of such. One may not understand the motivating factor, or the force behind a phenomenon, but to say it does not happen simply because it cannot be repeated on cue, is to be guilty of limited thinking. Thoughtful people set about trying to understand the how and why of the seemingly impossible, regardless of the jeers of the skeptics. They realize that many natural laws have been uncovered by people who persisted in the attempt to understand that which *could not happen but did!*

STIGMATA: CONTROVERSIAL PHENOMENON

The existence of stigmata is one of the most controversial of all phenomena. It is not one of my favorite enigmas, but it has excited comments by many important researchers; particularly, the case of the celebrated Therese Neumann of Konnersreuth. Books have been written about this stigmatist—not all concur that this is a genuine manifestation. It is an unalterable fact, however, that many people have agreed that this simple Bavarian peasant woman is exactly what she appears to be—a true stigmatist. It is also true that there have been attestations by apparently unimpeachable witnesses that she is also clairvoyant and has the gifts of healing and speaking in tongues as well. Another phenomenal claim made for this unusual woman is that she has had no solid food since 1922 and no liquids since 1927! As recently as 1953, a comprehensive study was made of this and was published in a book called *The Riddle of Konnersreuth,* by Paul Siwek.

Padre Pio, the Italian stigmatist, was visited by the eminent author and theologian, Dr. Marcus Bach. In his report of his visit, in the August 1963 issue of *Fate Magazine,* Dr. Bach clearly states that this was a genuine demonstration of the stigmata so far as he was concerned.

Who can possibly explain this bleeding which appears to be spontaneous at the same spots the body of the crucified Jesus Christ bled from his wounds? Many explanations have been put forth, but none seem to be satisfactory. Even though it appears to elude explanation or understanding, it is a phenomenon which must be real—thousands of people are willing to swear to it.

ESP POWERS OF INSECTS

Of more immediate reality to me are the amazing demonstrations of ESP (?) powers of insects and bugs. Some years ago a friend of mine, after reading an article in *The Reader's Digest* about some women who talked some spiders out of their home, decided to make a test of her own.

I was an interested observer for this initial attempt.

We went into her kitchen, a spot where tiny ants had plagued her for weeks. She explained, in a reasonable, conversational manner, directing her remarks to the stream of them on her sink, that she really did not want to do violence to them, but they really had no right to invade her home. She talked patiently to them for several minutes, and even as we stood looking at them the stream began to thin out noticeably. Within a half hour there was not a sign of an ant in her kitchen.

Since that time I have done the same thing—as have many of my friends. It really works—the exact explanation is unknown.

PLANT RESPONSES TO HUMAN ATTITUDES

Another interesting thought is the possibility that plants are just as responsive as insects to human attitudes toward them. The reports in *The Power of Prayer on Plants* by Franklin Loehr show conclusively that plants will respond to thought projection or verbalized communication. In a similar, or at least related, vein, a friend of mine surprised me one evening with an entirely new thought. She stated that she was sure she had the most psychic nut-grass in the state of Florida!

As the conversation progressed I realized that she was much more serious in her belief than I had at first thought. She said that when she would take hold of a piece of this weed to pull it out, the first tug would get it out without too much difficulty, but each piece would become increasingly resistant. She felt that weeds, not quickly and cleanly snatched out of the ground, in some way communicated with their nearby fellows, warning them of impending annihilation. She was convinced that each weed, once warned, clung to its place tenaciously; all of the weeds within reach seemed to be equally defiant, as if they conspired to make her job difficult.

A day or so later I told another gardening fan about this idea and, much to my surprise, she concurred with it! She said that had been her experience, too! Who knows? If plants respond to love and prayer, why not to the threat of danger?

SPONTANEOUS UNSEEN GUIDANCE

As a last ingredient in this mixture of miscellany, let me insert a few words about unseen guidance.

Is there anyone who has not felt the pull of invisible hands, "heard" unspoken words of warning, or gone to the right place at the right time with no forethought of his own? Surely a little reflection on the part of almost anyone will bring into focus such an experience.

That one person attributes this to guidance or protection from guardian spirits, another to the hand of God, coincidence or even instinct is not too important. The realization that no one has produced incontrovertible proof of the source of this manifestation does not in any way affect its reality.

That it does occur I do not doubt. To say "coincidence" is to take the easy way out. Free use of the "chance" explanation never produced the kind of analytical and observant mind that is behind every progressive accomplishment in the world in which we live.

This unseen force which guides us and protects us is, I believe, the same force which inspires and directs creative efforts, discoveries and inventions. Inspiration is just one of the facets of this unseen force. If one can accept it as a creative force, why split hairs about accepting it as a protective one?

SUMMARY OF CHAPTER FIFTEEN

1. There are many classifications and sub-classifications of psychic phenomena.
2. Records exist and continue to accumulate showing that people and objects disappear in inexplicable ways suggestive of spontaneous dematerialization.
3. Animals demonstrate a highly developed psychic sense.
4. Death-bed utterances and experiences during critical illness indicate survival of both the consciousness and personality after "death."
5. What we call the "past" seems to be still occurring in another dimension.
6. Many children have playmates seemingly visible and real to them, but imaginary or phantom to adults.
7. Instances of stigmata, although rare, have been documented by responsible observers.
8. Even plants have psychic sensitivity.
9. Unknown forces protect, guide and inspire us if we will psychically recognize them and use them for our best interests.